DESIGNING A COFFEEHOUSE

Branding

Coffee

Interior

A collection of creative
designs for coffeehouse

SP
SendPoints

DESIGNING A COFFEEHOUSE

©2020 SendPoints Publishing Co., Ltd.
First printing of the first edition, January 2020

SP
SendPoints

EDITED & PUBLISHED BY SendPoints Publishing Co., Ltd.

PUBLISHER: Lin Gengli

PUBLISHING DIRECTOR: Lin Shijian

CHIEF EDITOR: Lin Shijian

DESIGN ADVISOR: Chen Ting

EXECUTIVE EDITOR: Li Weiji

EXECUTIVE ART EDITOR: Chen Ting

PROOFREADING: Li Weiji

REGISTERED ADDRESS: Room 15A Block 9 Tsui Chuk Garden, Wong Tai Sin, Kowloon, Hong Kong

TEL: +852-35832323 / **FAX:** +852-35832448

OFFICE ADDRESS: 7F, 9th Anning Street, Jinshazhou, Baiyun District, Guangzhou, China

TEL: +86-20-89095121 / **FAX:** +86-20-89095206

BEIJING OFFICE: Flat 1701, Block C, BBMG International, Wangjing West Road no.48, Chaoyang District, Beijing, China

TEL: +86-10-84139071 / **FAX:** +86-10-84139071

SHANGHAI OFFICE: Room 302, Floor 3, Ningbo Road no.349, Huangpu District, Shanghai, China

TEL: +86-21-63523469 / **FAX:** +86-21-63523469

SALES TEAM

UK, Europe, Africa, Oceania: Sunnie sales02@sendpoints.cn

America, the Middle East: Mia sales03@sendpoints.cn

Asia: Hedy sales01@sendpoints.cn

TEL: +86-20-81007895

EMAIL: sales@sendpoints.cn

WEBSITE: www.sendpoints.cn / www.spbooks.cn

ISBN 978-988-79284-5-4

BRANDING

P4~99

THE ASSEMBLY STORE

1

2

Kuppa

COFFEE

EST. 2006

AS IT SHOULD BE

COFFEE AS IT SHOULD BE

ESTD 2006

KUPPA

ROASTERY & CAFÉ

3

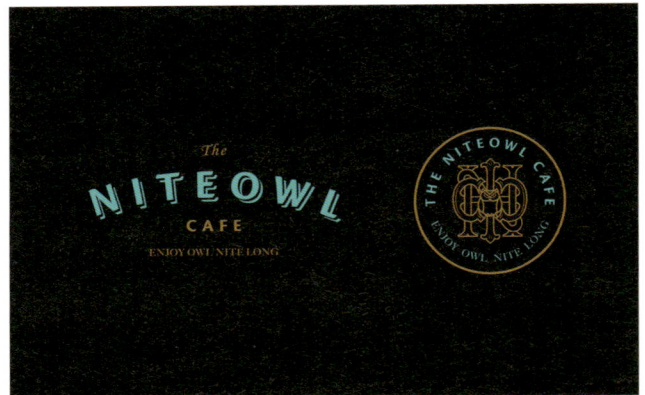

4

5

1. Studio：Bravo，Design：Jasmine Lee | 2. Studio：MAROG Creative Agency，Design：Siranush Danielyan, Varduhi Antonyan, Haykaz Khroyan

3. Studio：Serious Studio，Design：Tintin Lontoc, Deane Miguel, Lester Cruz, Claudine Santos | 4. Design：ZiYu Ooi | 5. Studio：Lemongraphic，Design：Rayz Ong

CAFÉ

Chiquilín

BAR & SPEISEN

6

NORD
— COFFEE
ROASTERY

7

8

9

COFFEE MASTERS™

10

HÊRMANN
THÔMAS

COFFEE MASTERS™

6. Studio : ADDA Studio . Design : Christian Vogtlin | 7. Studio : Cumba Co . Design : Kutan Ural | 8. Design : Carla Almeida | 9. Studio : Lilkudley . Design : Petr Kudlacek
10. Studio : mxTAD . Design : Merche C. Esnal, Adolfo Meneses, Mr. Power, Fe-nanda Miranda, Monir Jimenez, Mauricio Romero

11

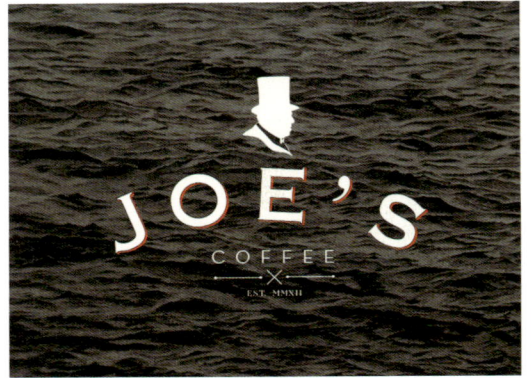

12

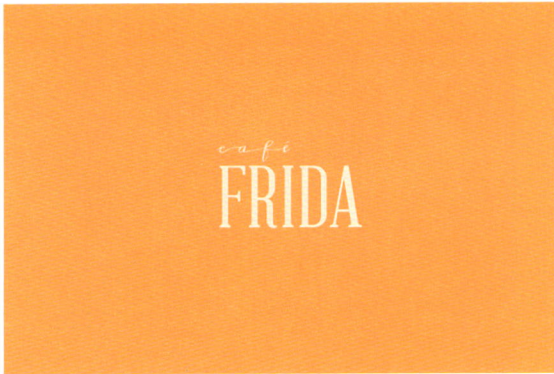

13

14

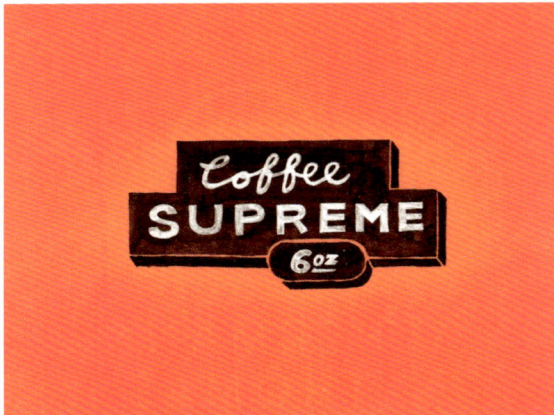

15

16

11. Design：Mustafa Akülker | 12. Studio：Revert Design，Design：Trevor Finnegan | 13. Design：Marie-Michelle Dupuis, Pier-Luc Cossette | 14. Studio：Logomachine，
Design：Arina Rudyakova | 15. Studio：Hardhat，Design：Nik Clifford, Jenny Miles | 16. Studio：One Plus One Design，Design：Tyler Thiessen, Jessie Thiessen

17

19

18

20

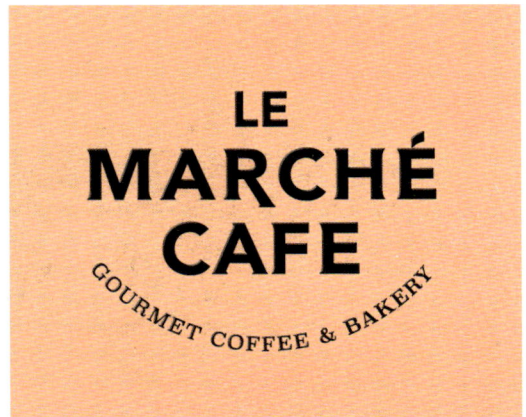

21

17. Studio：Bond Creative Agency，Design：Jesper Bange, James Zambra ｜ 18. Studio：Ostecx Créative，Design：Sébastien Ploszaj ｜ 19. Studio：Estudio Yeᴉé

20. Studio：Reynolds & Reyner，Design：Alexander Andreyev, Artyom Kulik ｜ 21. Design：Jiani Lu

As one of the most common beverages world wide, coffee even forms its own rich cultural atmosphere. With the improvement of living style, specialty coffee brands born in the third wave of coffee are striving to distinguish themselves from others through branding.

Generally, coffee brands prefer to choose visual elements that are close to coffee itself. The raw materials (coffee beans, coffea), coffee makers (moka pot), coffee wares (ceramic cup, takeaway cup, creamer pot), even coffee stains are the most commonly used elements. Some branding is inspired by the customs and culture of the countries where their beans are sourced. Since coffee shops are not only serving coffee nowadays, pastries (donut, croissant, omlet) are linked to the coffee. In Western culture, a new day starts from a cup of coffee, so objects like the sun, smile, milk bottle are also involved sometimes.

ORYGYNS Specialty Coffee

Kuppa Roastery & Café

Bronuts

Visual elements directly linked to coffee are classic ones, but they could be a bit dull; a competitive market requires more unique branding. Therefore, the use of vintage objects of historical meaning is another branding inclination.

During the Age of Discovery, coffee was spread across the world as people sailed toward the unknown. Elements like sailing ship, anchor, sailor are often seen in coffee branding. The first Industrial revolution renovated the world drastically during 19th century. Being the best representations of this era, steam engine, bicycle, neon light, phonograph, camera can always add a sense of historical connotation to the branding. The turbulent 20th century gave birth to numerous renowned masters who hung out with talented people at cafés, making cafés a place filled with humanity. Thus, beard, tobacco pipe, gentleman, tie, bowler hat, book, glasses, Greek mythological figures, cat, music and so on are used.

Last but not least, from the perspective of general branding, coffee brands like brands of other products tend to choose an animal to convey their values. Based on general cultural context, these animals are the mostly applied ones: owl (wisdom and mystery), elephant (caring and tolerance), cock (enthusiasm and resolution), stag (protection and guide), unicorn (spirituality and nature), fox (naughtiness and guile), lion (masculinity and bravery).

It is a very efficient way to use the image of animals in branding, because animals are regarded as something with human traits thanks to fairy tales and myths. The branding for Hêrmann Thômas uses antlers to suggest masculinity, while rabbit ears implies femininity.

Unicorn is described as a mythical creature that could only be captured by a virgin, and therefore, is a symbol of purity and grace. The funny part is that the designers go against this stereotype by placing a fork on the unicorn's forehead instead of the usual spiraling horn, resulting in a playful and rebellious brand image.

Voltacafé

Calle 20 #235, Local 107, Mérida, Yucatán, México

Studio : BIENAL

Voltacafé is a homage to the yesteryear's cafés, a space for "tertulias"—informal intellectual gatherings. It aims to rescue traditional coffee culture and preserve space for dialogue and culture, thus adapting the elegance and quality of the olden days to our times. The feeling of nostalgia and intelligentsia in its branding is represented by nature-inspired strokes, elegant color palette, and custom-made pattern. The logo mark is composed of two cups that join to form the letter "V" and three circles, where the central one is carried by two carrier pigeons. The circles represent a safe place for communication and knowledge. The logotype has also contributed to the antique style with its strong strokes and classic geometric serifs.

VOLTACAFÉ

C	60%	R	61%	
M	60%	G	53%	
Y	65%	B	48%	
K	60%			

C	07%	R	222%	
M	85%	G	77%	
Y	79%	B	64%	
K	01%			

C	20%	R	178%	
M	41%	G	135%	
Y	67%	B	90%	
K	15%			

C	05%	R	239%	
M	05%	G	235%	
Y	08%	B	228%	
K	00%			

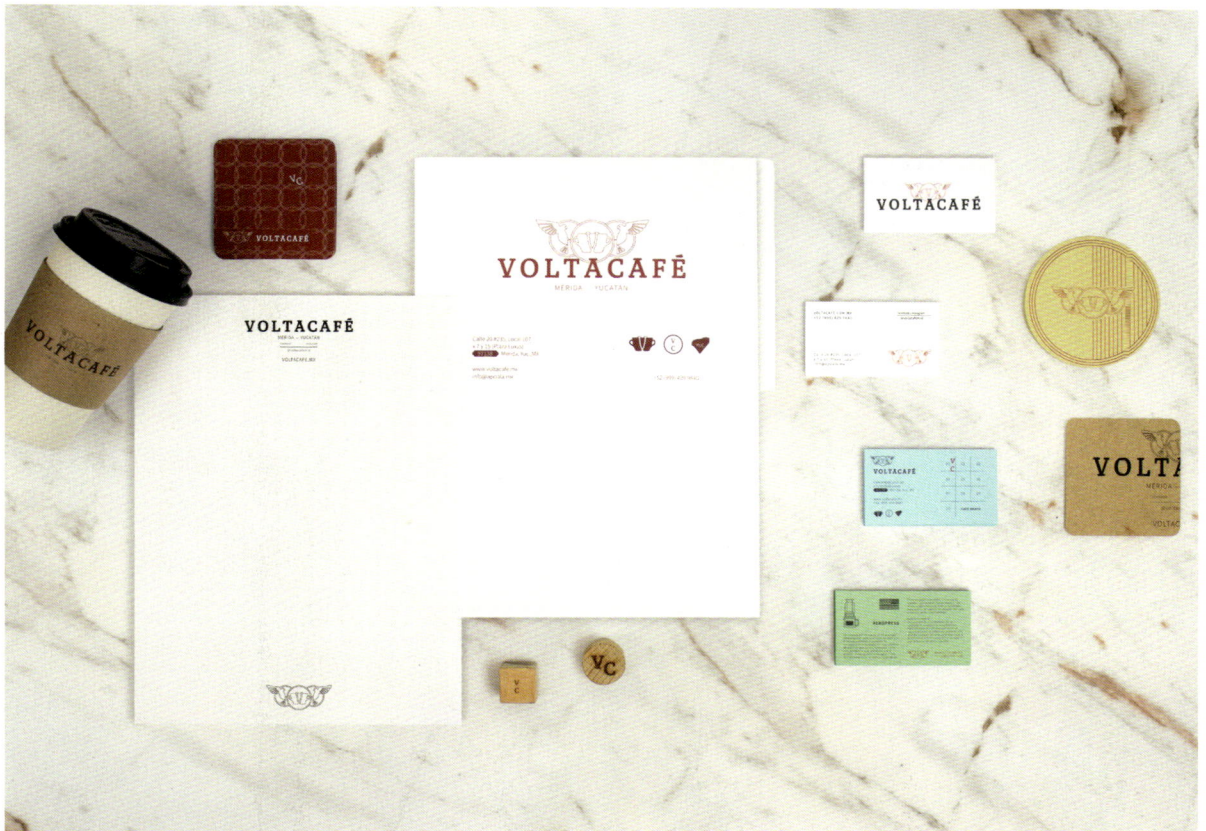

Granger

49A Grange Road, Caulfield East 3145, Australia

Studio : Mildred & Duck

Named after Grange Road on which it sits, Granger is a neighborhood-focused venture, a regular haunt for locals. Thus its visual identity was created to be approachable with an enduring relaxed elegance, in harmony with the materials and colors used in the interior. Using a palette of creams and warm whites, punctuated with the signature green used in the fit-out, the designers utilized quietly understated finishes such as white foiling to echo the confident restraint of the space itself.

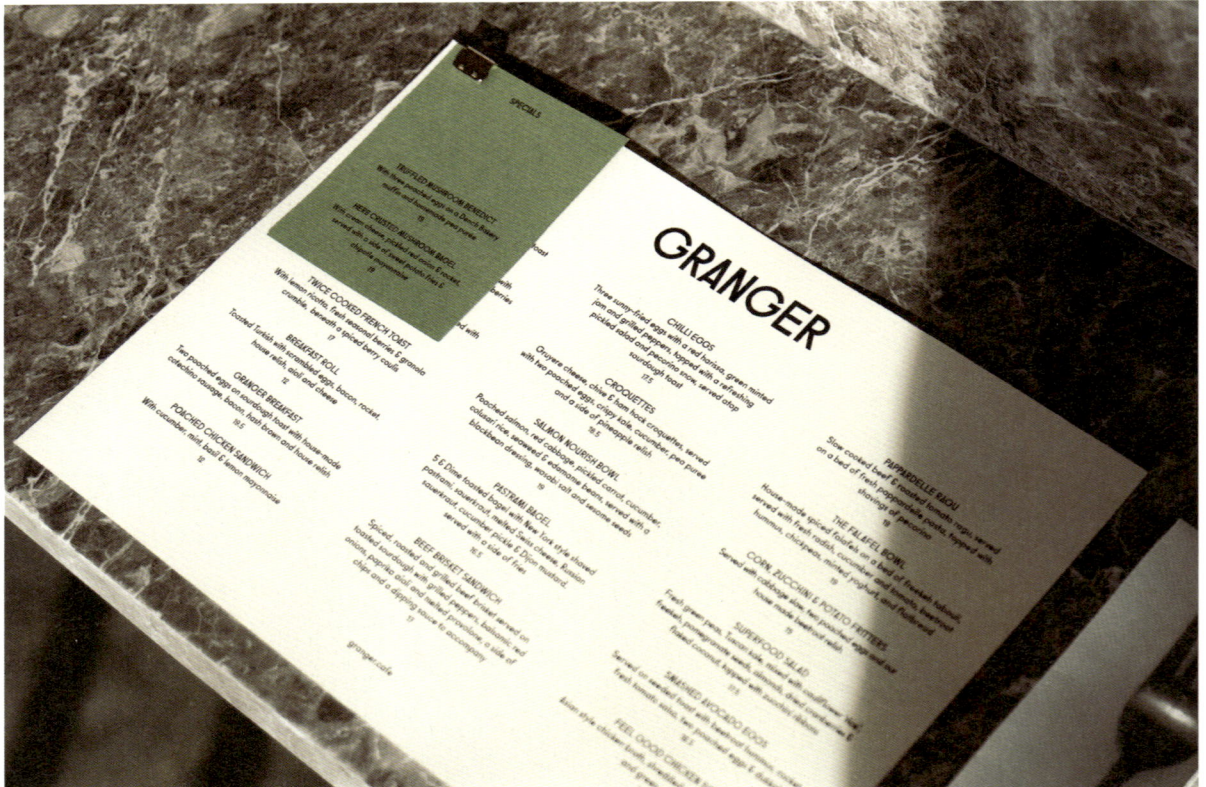

White Glass Coffee

23−18 Sakuragaokacho, Shibuya City, Tokyo, Japan

Studio : Emuni

Design : So Nagai

Located in the city of Shibuya, this is a coffee shop with the concept "roaster in the forest". The logo symbolizes the space which is surrounded by green plants and talks with nature, as well as the time that people spend happily in this space. The overlap is the shape of a glass, revealing the concept of the brand name, which is also reflected in the packaging design of coffee beans, jars, cups, donut boxes and wrapping paper.

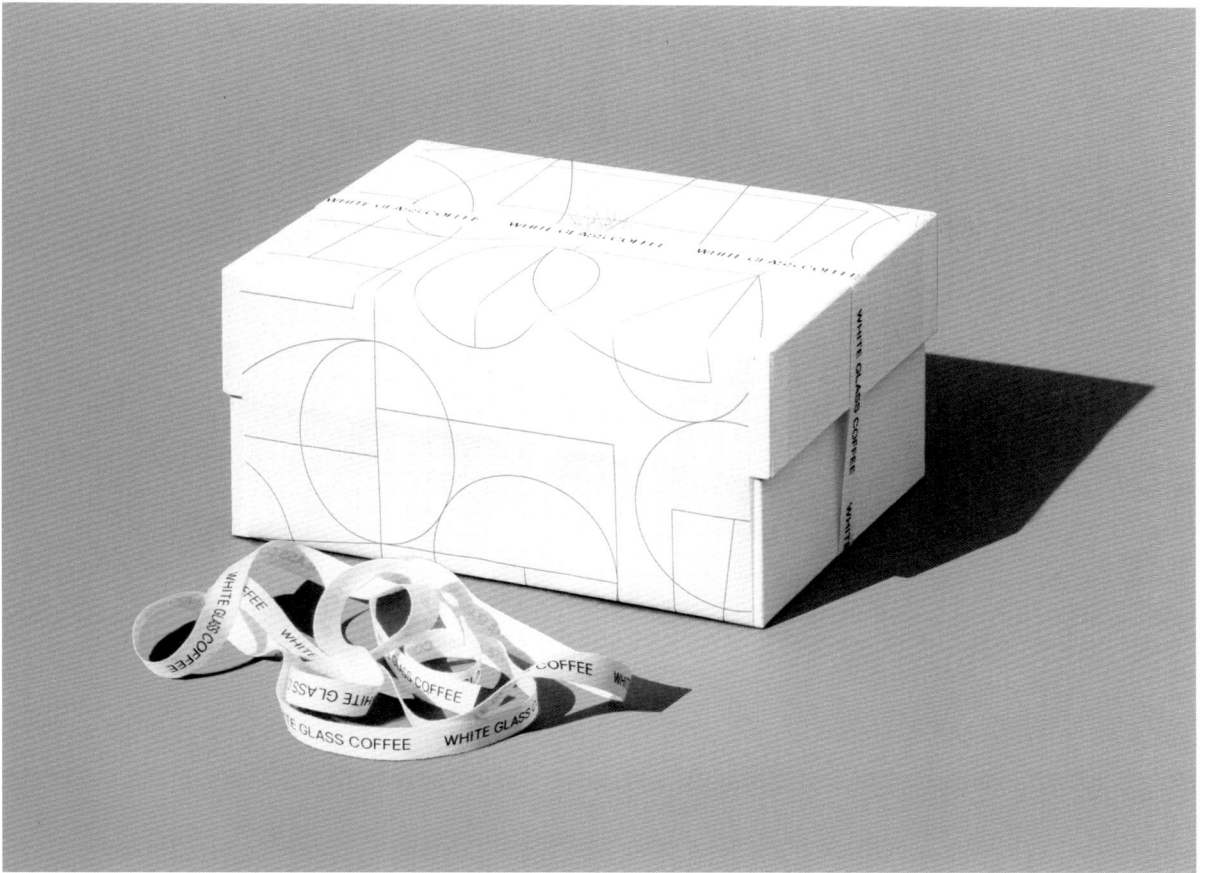
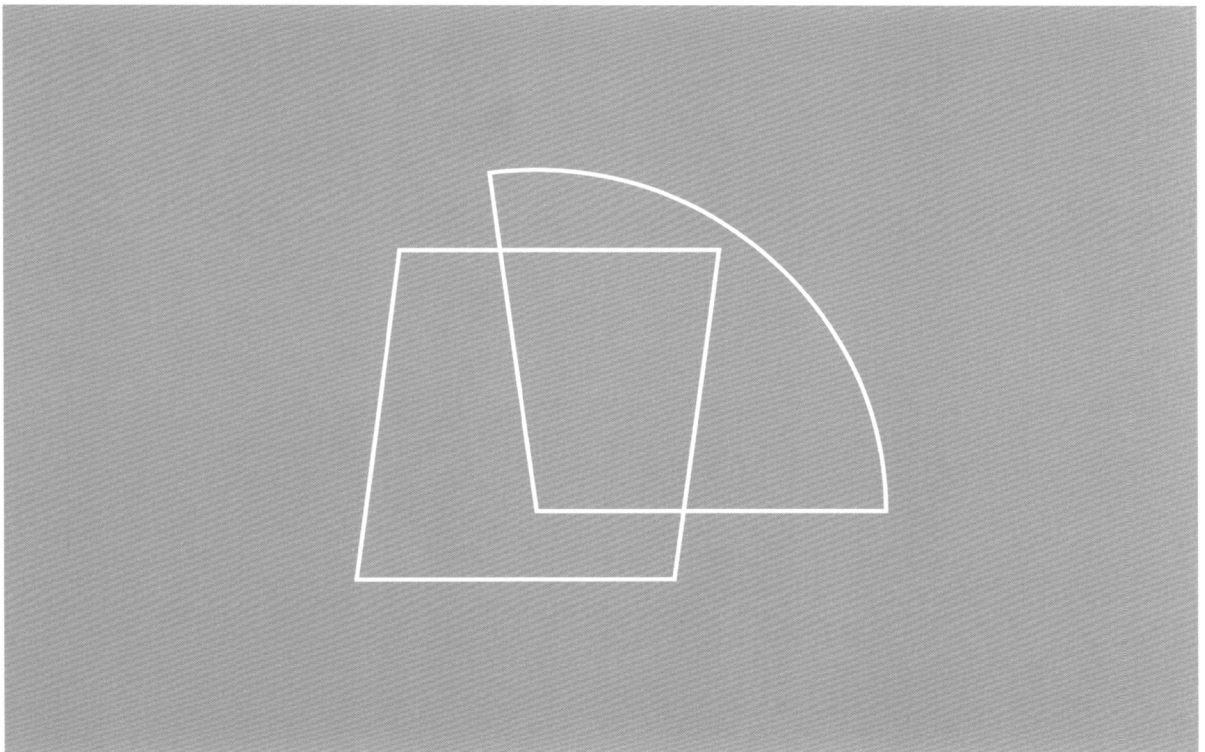

Co. Means Coffee

Nezalezhnosti Avenue, 10 A , Kharkiv, Kharkiv Oblast, Ukraine

Studio : Canape Agency

Design : Daria Stetsenko

Co. Means Coffee is a pet friendly cafe in the business center of the city. The brand name is phonetically associated with coffee, cocoa or company, so cobalt blue and image of the cow are used throughout the branding. Additionally, the cow symbolizes the animal friendly orientation of the cafe and adds an image of fun and home comfort. Blue color has been complemented with warm shades of pink and ocher, and the cow depicted as simply and calmly as possible. The logotype consists of both serif and sans-serif fonts, hinting at the restrained character and the youth of the brand.

Co.
MEANS COFFEE

info@coffee.co.ua

Харьков,
пр-т Правды, 10а
+38 050 423 25 26

COFFEE.CO.UA

Co.
COFFEE
COCOA
COW

Харьков, пр-т Правды, 10а
+38 099 40 11 000 | info@coffee.co.ua

Co.
MEANS   COFFEE

07:30—22:00

SEVEN DAYS
A WEEK

Co.
MEANS
COFFEE
Papua New Guinea
Typica, Arusha
Washed
1550 м
Долина Vagi
Kigabah
Насыщенный фруктовый аромат с нотами вишни
Сочная сладость сливы и крыжовника
Чернослив, орех
Среднее
Bunna
Папуа Новая Гвинея, Бразилия
и Колумбия
Сухофрукты, изюм, гвоздика и корица
Цитрусовый вкус, с нотами лайма,
сливы и корицы
Долгое сливочное
Плотное
Columbia Excelso
Catura
Washed
1300–1900 м
Pitalito, Huila
Цитрусы, ржаной хлеб
Вино, фрукты, тростниковый сахар
Легкое, сладкое
Среднее
Honduras Bella Vista
Catual Rojo
Natural
1500–1600 м
Sata Rosa de Copan
Орех, карамель, вяленая вишня
Корица, шоколад, апельсин
Сладкое, черный шоколад
Плотное
Ethiopia Yirgacheffe Gr.2
Typica
Washed
1770–2200 м
Yirgacheffe
Цитрусы, виноград, лайм и бергамот
Черный чай с лимоном, ежевика, абрикосовая
косточка и сладкие цитрусы
Яркая цитрусовая свежесть и сладость
Среднее
Guatemala Coban
Cattura, Catual
Washed
1300–1500 м
Coban
Специи, яблоко
Цитрусы, карамель, ваниль
Сладкое, карамель
Плотное
Brazil Santos
Catura, Catual
Natural
200–800 м
Minas Gerais Sao Paulo
Шоколад, орех
Игристое вино, шоколад, жасмин
Долгое, корка жареного хлеба
Плотное
Ethiopia Aricha
Mixed variates
Natural
1950–2100 м
Yirgacheffe, район Gedeo
Aricha
Яркий ягодно-фруктовый аромат
с нотами малины и ежевики
Ягодный сироп, малина и вишня
Яркая сладость, легкая кислинка
с горчинкой какао
Среднее
Kenya Ruka Chui
SL28, SL34
Washed
1600–2000 м
Nyeri
Сочный аромат черной
смородины и сухофрукты
Насыщенная цитрусовая кислинка,
терпкость грейпфрута и мандарин
Цветочно-жасминовые оттенки
и чай с бергамотом
Среднее
Black Velvet
Колумбия, Эфиопия
и Гватемала
Чистый, сбалансированный,
ноты гречишного меда, клюквы
и чая с бергамотом
Цветочный мед, кардамон, бергамот
Мягкое и сладкое
Округлое

Co. MEANS COFFEE
info@coffee.co.ua
ПРИХОДИ
С ДРУГОМ!
ОТКРЫТИЕ
PETS FRIENDLY
КОФЕЙНИ
В ХАРЬКОВЕ
ПРОСПЕКТ
ПРАВДЫ, 10а
ВОЗЛЕ МЕТРО
УНИВЕРСИТЕТ
+38 099 40 11 000
COFFEE.CO.UA

27

The Roasters

547-6 Okawachi, Wakayama, 640-0316, Japan

Studio：Emuni

Design：Masashi Murakami, Moe Shibata

Specialty coffee of The Roasters are roasted according to the characteristics of the producing country, and are sold wholesale around Japan. Each country's unique customs are translated into colours and shapes, representing it's characteristics. The packaging were developed by line drawing based on different countries.

Café Michelena

Allende 199-247, Centro Histórico de Morelia, 58000 Morelia, Mich., Mexico

Studio : Henriquez Lara Estudio

Design : Javier Henriquez Lara, Pablo Salazar Correa, Lorena Sanchez Aldana, Ivan Soto Camba

Café Michelena is a bookstore and coffeehouse at Morelia downtown. This is a brand that celebrates the link between books, great conversations, history, and coffee. The branding was inspired by the historical figure Mariano de Michelena, a precursor of the Mexican independence and the person who first introduced coffee to Mexico. Michelena was probably the first Mexican to enjoy a book and a coffee at the same time. A series of vintage-style illustrations act as the main visual element to generate the early 19th-century vibe.

The Assembly Ground

2 Handy Road, #01-21 The Cathay, Singapore 229233

Studio : Bravo

Design : Jasmine Lee

The Assembly is a lifestyle store targeted at men's fashion. To provide a place for customers to have a rest when shopping, a cafe called The Assembly Ground was opened. The identity for the café is classic, versatile and playful. The logo mark relates to the initial of the brand name and the color palette is a selection of highly saturated colors which can be mixed and matched for variation.

STORE STACKED LOGO

THE
ASSEMBLY
STORE

CAFE STACKED LOGO

THE
ASSEMBLY
GROUND

STORE HORIZONTAL LOGO

THE △ ASSEMBLY

MONOGRAM

CHICKENWIRE

GINGHAM

CHECKERED

SIMPLIFIED
HOUNDSTOOTH

PINSTRIPE

STRIPES

DIAMOND

HERRINGBONE

WAVE

SANDWICH

ORANGE
143U

SALAD

GREEN
3278U

DESSERT

RED
177U

OTHERS

YELLOW
128U

The ASSEMBLY
BY BENJAMIN BARKER

THE ASSEMBLY
• BENJAMIN BARKER •

THE ASSEMBLY

THE
ASSEMBLY
STORE

THE
ASSEMBLY
CLOTHIER & CO
BENJAMIN BARKER

A
THE ASSEMBLY
Store

THE ASSEMBLY
★ ★ ★
BY BENJAMIN BARKER

THE
ASSEMBLY
STORE & CAFE
★ ★ ★

THE
ASSEMBLY
STORE

THE
ASSEMBLY
CAFE

ASSEMBLY.

The
ASSEMBLY
· Store ·
BENJAMIN BARKER

THE ASSEMBLY

BLY
MIN BARKER

BLY

LY

MBLY
**

THE ASSEMBLY
BACKSTAGE

THE
ASSEMBLY
GENERAL STORE
· BENJAMIN BARKER ·

THE
ASSEMBLY
Store

THE ASSEMBLY
Store

THE *assembly* STORE

THE ASSEMBLY
★★★   ★★★
STORE AND CAFE

Some of the logos designed in the course of identity development.

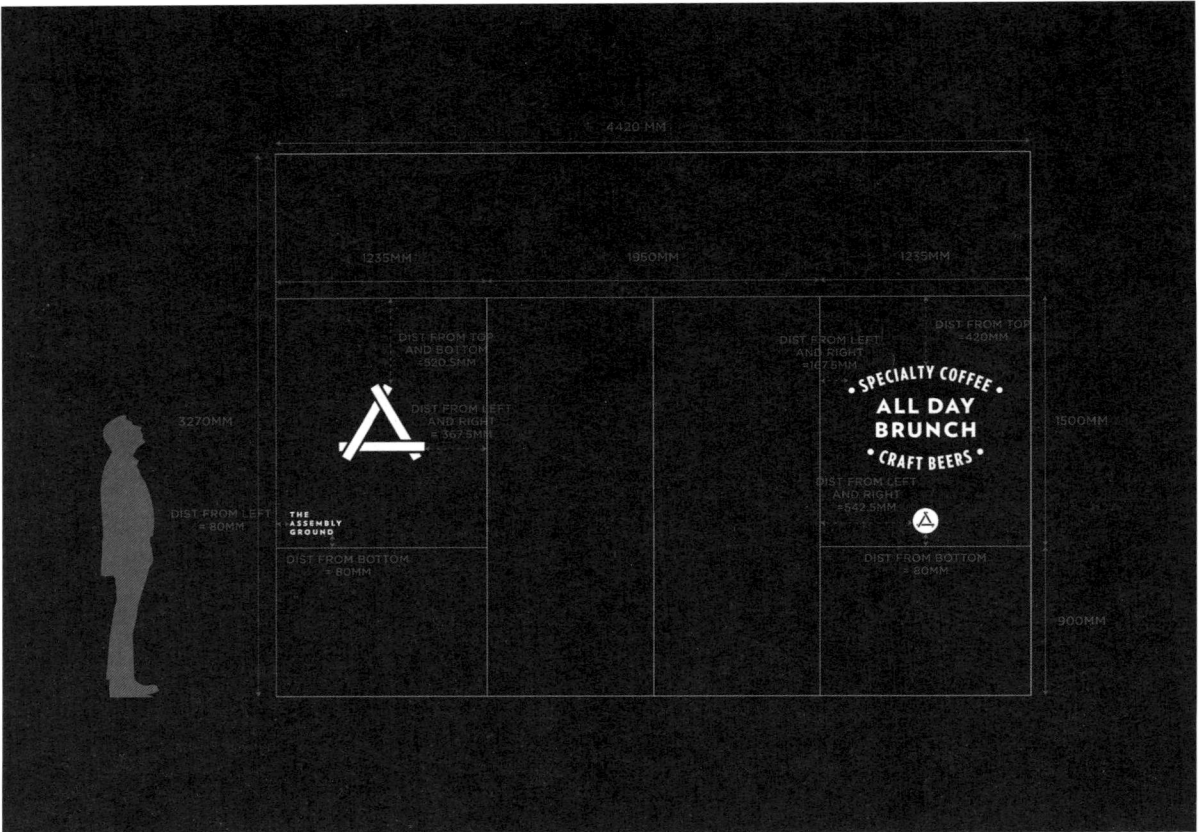

4420 MM

1235MM · 1960MM · 1235MM

3270MM

DIST FROM TOP AND BOTTOM =520.5MM

DIST FROM LEFT AND RIGHT = 367.5MM

THE ASSEMBLY GROUND

DIST FROM LEFT = 80MM

DIST FROM BOTTOM = 80MM

DIST FROM LEFT AND RIGHT =1675MM

DIST FROM TOP =420MM

1500MM

· SPECIALTY COFFEE ·
ALL DAY BRUNCH
· CRAFT BEERS ·

DIST FROM LEFT AND RIGHT =542.5MM

DIST FROM BOTTOM = 80MM

900MM

WIDTH = 280MM
HEIGHT = 380MM

THE
ASSEMBLY
STORE

London Coffee House

Verkhnii Val St, 18, Kyiv, Ukraine

Studio : Reynolds & Reyner

Design : Alexander Andreyev, Artyom Kulik

London is a city deeply rooted in its traditions, history and architecture. Loyalty and good manners are the qualities that Londoners are most proud of. Accordingly, the designers strive to weave these cultural assets into the branding. The logo was incorporated with the crown which represents dignity. The purple color and Burberry-like grids endow the whole visuals a sense of British elegance.

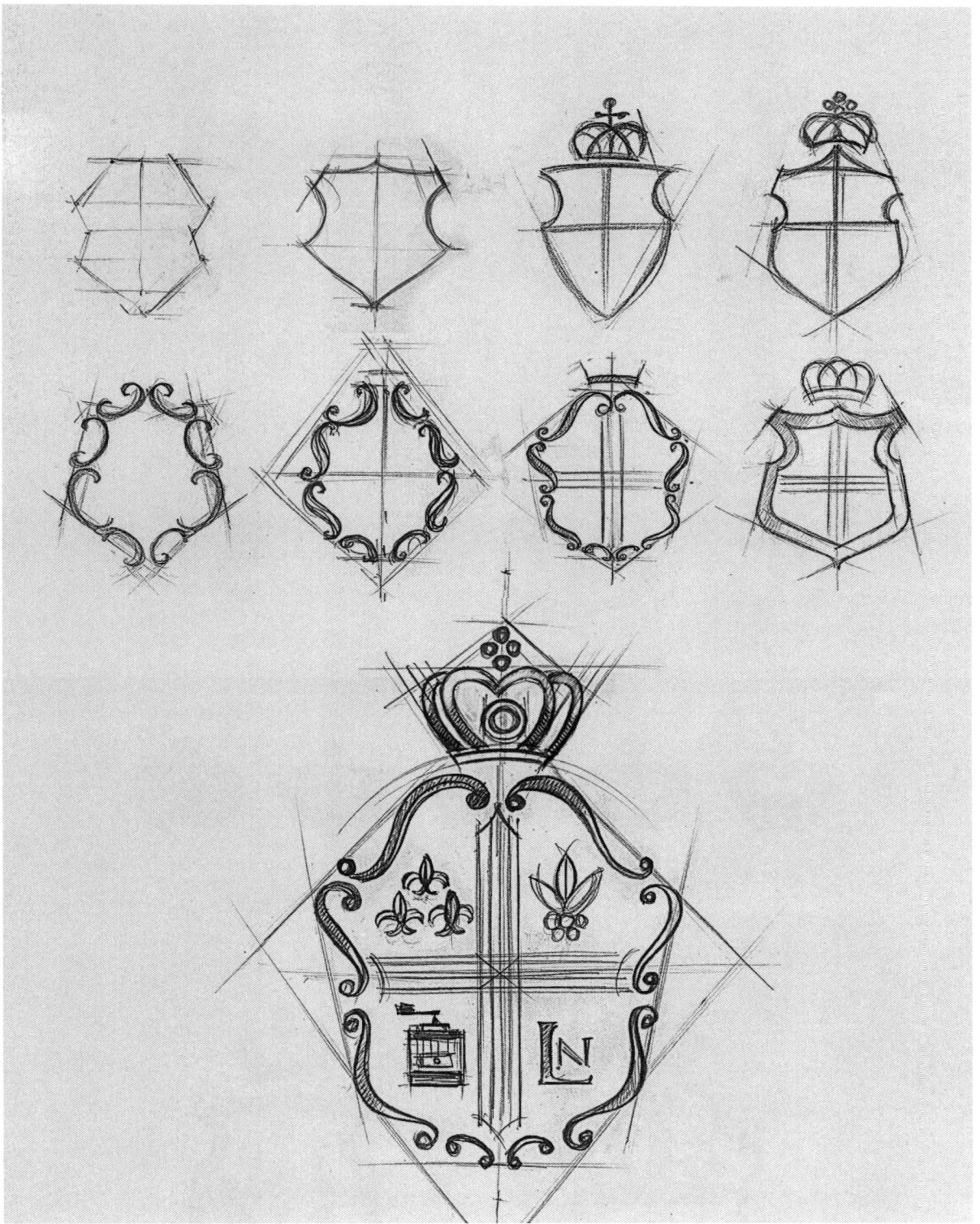

Вариант   5. Best   3. Толщина

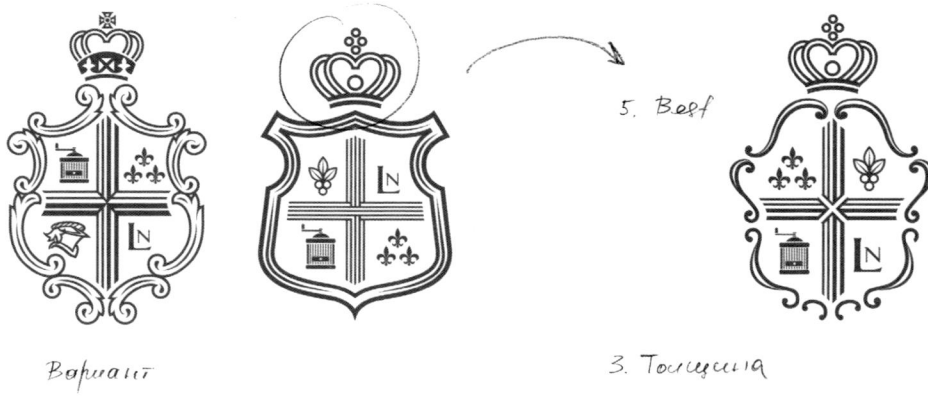

Вариант   5. Best   3. Толщина

3. Корона   5. Best

4. Лучший   3. Корона

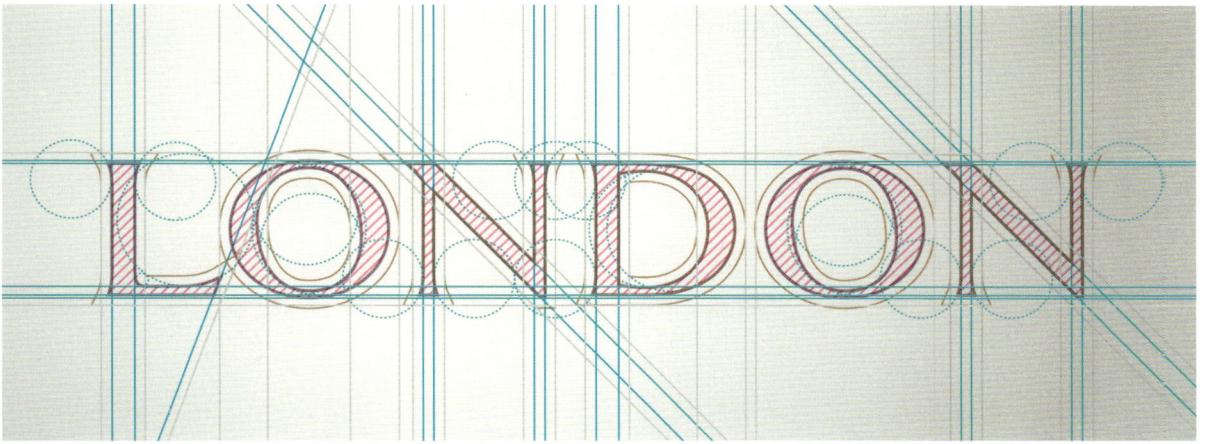

Café Diego

Nation Galleria, Al Khubeirah, Abu Dhabi, United Arab Emirates

Studio : Backbone Branding

Design : Stepan Azaryan, Narek Matevosyan

Located in Abu Dhabi, Café Diego was developed to create a public space of Argentine style. As one of the most well-known symbols of Argentina, the image of the legendary football player Diego Armando Maradona was incorporated into the identity to recall the colorful Argentinian backstreets, architecture and street art. The packaging was specially developed for takeaway coffee: thin, easy-to-fold, and oil-proof.

Cofix

34 Weizman St., Kfar Saba, 4424712 Israel

Studio : Kapsoola

Design : Anna Geslev, Rona Fromer

Cofix is an Israeli coffee chain known for its fair, fixed priced product: only 5 NIS for each product, which has revolutionized the Israeli café market. The designers chose a catchy brand name and the sharp contrast of black-and-white palette, all combined in a minimalistic, functional, straightforward visual language that communicates an affordable, confident image.

cofix
fresh coffee. fixed price
take away
cofix cofix cofix cofix
good morning! good morning
take away take away
pastry pastry pastry
FRESH COFFEE FIXED PRICE
HELLO!
Take Me Away
FRESH STUFF
HAVE A GOOD MORNING!
TAKE AWAY / TAKE AWAY
FRESH SNACKS FIXED PRICE

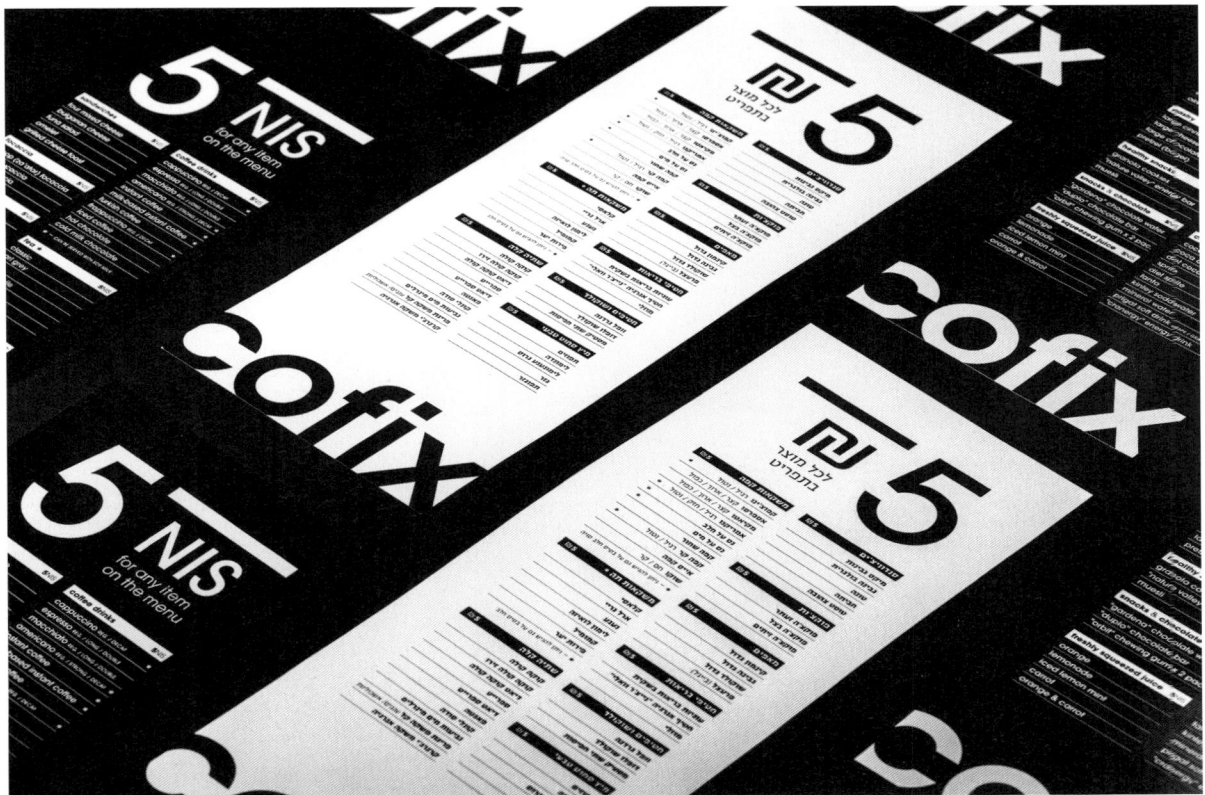

8 Pizza

275 Thomson Road, #01-02 Novena Regency, Singapore

Studio : Lemongraphic

Design : Rayz Ong

8 Pizza is a Singaporean restaurant serving eight kinds of speciality pizzas. The number "8" in the logotype was inspired by the moving trajectory of making a pizza with dough, and the lettering of "PIZZA" resembles the tableware used in the restaurant. Its coffee is made specifically to go with the pizzas. The style was built upon a retro graphic basis, conveying the image of the brand: classic yet original.

8 PIZZA

MENU

The Beginning

Antipasto **18.00**

Egg Plant Casserole **9.90**

Bruschetta **10.90**

Caesar Salad with Chicken and Crouton **8.90**

Braised Meat Ball w Chorizo and Cheese **14.90**

Hand Cut French Fries w Truffle Béarnaise **10.00**

Light Mushroom Soup with Puff Pastry **7.00**

Nutty Pumpkin Soup **6.00**

Garlic Bread **3.00**

OUR SIGNATURE
Flavors OF THE WORLD

TRIPLE CHEESE "COMFORT" 16.00
Cheddar | Camembert | Emmental | Vine Fresh Cherry Tomato | Cured Ham

TROPICAL "THOUGHTS" 14.00
Pineapple | Pepperoni | Marinated Feta with Thyme oil | Caramelized Swee
| Arugula | Light Lemon Cream Cheese

SEAFOOD "STEW" ON FLAT BREAD 18.00
Crabmeat | Mussel | Bacon & Onion | Yuzu Emulsion | Aged Bonito | Seawe

TRUFFLE "SCENTED" ON EARTH 20.00
Truffle Soft Scramble | Corn | Cabbage | Smoked Salmon | Seaweed dressing |

ROASTED CHICKEN "SRIRACHA" 16.00
Roasted Chicken | Red Pepper Jam | Chilli Powder | Ginger | Crushed Moz
| Lime Sour Cream

BEEF AND MUSHROOM "FOREST" IN WILDERNESS 2
Mince Beef Ball | Mushroom Stew | Masala | Chilli | Lime | Crushed Tomato
| Spinach | Yoghurt "Cheddar" Glaze

BACK TO THE FUTURE "PISSALADIERE" UNFORGOTTEN MEM
Mozzarella | Braised Onion | Green Olive | Parsley

9 MONTHS (VINEGAR) CHEEK 26.00
Braised Beef Cheek | Aged Balsamic Vinegar | Baby Spinach | Burned Bu
| Pommery Mustard | BBQ Glaze

PIZZA

Create Your own Pizza

STEP 01
Choose your sauces

STEP 02
Choose your ingredients

STEP 03
Choose your Topping

STEP 04
Waiting Time 15mins

Start from

12.00

ADDITIONAL TOPPING 120GM

Chicken	3.00	Pepperoni	5.00
Beef	5.00	Truffle Oil	2.00
Seafood	4.00		

Chilled Pasta

SAKURA 12.00
Seaweed | Sesame Dressing

TUNA 10.00
Sweet Pepper | Yuzu Dressing

SALMON ROE 12.00
Cucumber | Egg | Tomato | Dill | Prickled Vegetables

SMOKED SALMON 14.00
Sour Cream | Garlic Chip

Hot Pasta

PULLED PORK 14.00
Pork Stock | Garlic Cream

BRAISED BEEF 18.00
Pickled Baby Onion | Prosciutto Ham

SMOKED DUCK 15.00
Corn | Parsley

SEA URCHIN 22.00
Crab | Egg | Chive

BEVERAGE

Hot Coffee

ESPRESSO	3.50
DOUBLE ESPRESSO	4.00
ESPRESSO MACCHIATO	3.80
LONG BLACK	4.50
PICCOLO LATTE	4.50
CAPPUCCINO	5.00
FLAT WHITE	5.00
CAFFE LATTE	5.00
CAFFE MOCHA	5.50
AFFOGATO	6.00

Iced Coffee

ICED LONG BLACK	5.00
ICED LATTE	5.50
ICED CAPPUCCINO	5.50
ICED MOCHA	5.50

Tea

GRYPHON TEA	5.00

Additional

ESPRESSO	1.00
SOYMILK	1.00
HOT / ICE CHOCOLATE	4.50

Hêrmann Thômas Coffee Masters

Calle 2 (Avs. 1 y 3), 94500 Córdoba, Veracruz, México

Studio : mxTAD

Design : Merche C. Esnal, Adolfo Meneses, Mr. Power, Fernanda Miranda, Monir Jimenez, Mauricio Romero

Phil Hêrmann and Bree Thômas created an inspirational café, a space full of specialized books on architecture, design, cuisine and so on. Based on the image of the couple founders, the designers came up with two characters: Mr. Deer and Mrs. Rabbit. The elegant logo was developed by abstracting the characters' features (the antlers and the rabbit's ears) and combining the initials of the brand name (H and T). The space reacts to all of the visual elements, complementing the ideal atmosphere and the carefully planned dining experience.

COFFEE MASTERS™

HÊRMANN
THÔMAS
COFFEE MASTERS™

Kaldi Café

Victoria 309, Centro, Zona Centro, 31000 Chihuahua, Chih., Mexico

Studio : Estudio Yeyé

Kaldi is a coffee house that has been in the business for ten years. The brand identity incorporated the Greek elements into a series of Egyptian style illustrations to recall the historical awareness of ancient culture. The whole visual design portrays the café's belief in serving a good cup of coffee.

CH M G
CHOCOLATE CALIENTE 33 37 41
KALDI KID 30
MASALA CHAI LATTE 33 37 41
TÉ LATTE 33 37 41
G
CAPPUCCINO FRAPPE 40
MOKA FRAPPE 45
CARAMELO FRAPPE 48
KALDI FRAPPE 49
LATTE ROCKS 40
G
CHOCOLATE FRAPPE 43
TÉ FRIO 40
CHAI FRAPPE 45
SODA ITALIANA 40

Swing Coffee

1F., No.65, Songjiang Rd., Zhongshan Dist., Taipei City 104, Taiwan, China

Studio : Transform Design

Swing Coffee is a coffee shop located in Taipei. The logo is based on the word "swing" which subtly suggests coffee's fragrance. The brown tone emphasizes its calmness and cozy atmosphere, and the slogan "Good Things Take Time" represents the brand's belief in specialty coffee.

MINIMUM PRINT SIZE

S | CLEAR SPACE

15mm

7mm

5mm

SLOGAN

GOOD THINGS TAKE TIME
100%

GOOD THINGS TAKE TIME
70%

GOOD THINGS TAKE TIME
50%

APPLICATION TYPOGRAPHY

Aa

Aa

拾運
商行

DIN Cond
Light | **Medium**
ABCDEFGHIJKLMNOPQRSTUVWXYZ
abcdefghijklmnopqrstuvwxyz
0123456789

Avenir Next
Ultra Light | Regular | Medium | Demi Bold | **Bold** | **Heavy**
ABCDEFGHIJKLMNOPQRSTUVWXYZ
abcdefghijklmnopqrstuvwxyz
0123456789

華康儷黑
細黑 | 中黑 | 粗黑
主要標題及任何強調之中文文字請使用此字系列編排
英文、數字、符號或其他語言文字請使用英文字形。

STANDDARD COLOURS

AUXILIARY COLOURS

標準色 A	標準色 B	主要輔助色 C	主要輔助色 D	次要輔助色 E
PANTONE NEUTRAL BLACK U	PANTONE 466 U	PANTONE 7690 U	PANTONE 7401 U	PANTONE ORANGE 021 U
C73 M68 Y68 K28	C28 M38 Y52 K0	C74 M47 Y25 K0	C1 M14 Y42 K0	C0 M71 Y77 K0
R76 G72 B69	R197 G164 B126	R76 G126 B165	R255 G228 B163	R255 G108 B44

品牌顏色使用比例規範
由於品牌顏色較多為了維持品牌調性
的一致性，使用品牌色彩時請參照以
下色彩使用比例。

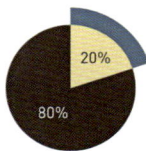

20%
80%

任一標準色A或B +
任一主要輔色C或D

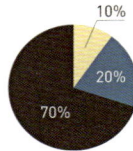

10%
20%
70%

任一標準色A或B +
雙主要輔色C和D

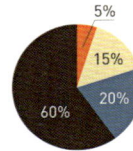

5%
15%
20%
60%

任一標準色A或B +
雙主要輔色C和D +
次主要輔色E

BACKGROUND COLOURS

為了避免品牌標誌與背景的應用上發
生識別度不清的問題，使用時請務必
遵守品牌標誌與背景色的規範，同時
也請注意保持品牌標誌的識別與清晰
度。最後，品牌標誌均不可使用於過
於複雜的背景上。

Coffee Supreme

52 Tyler Street, Britomart, Auckland, New Zealand

Studio : Hardhat

Design : Nik Clifford, Jenny Miles

Coffee Supreme is one of the largest independent coffee roasters and suppliers in New Zealand. This rebranding by Hardhat communicates its hand-crafted attention to detail and love of great coffee, as well as its approachable, supportive and friendly attitude. The new branding uses many hand-drawn illustrations and a strong color palette to stress the brand's reliability and professionalism.

Coffee SUPREME 6oz

1 KG

TOP STORY

WEIGHT ONE KILOGRAM

KG

111

FIND US

TO:

3 KG
COFFEE SUPREME

COFFEE SUPREME

THREE

ROASTED DAILY COFFEE SUPREME

SINGLE ORIGIN
ETHIOPIAN
YIRGACHEFFE
FAIR TRADE
ORGANIC

WITH COMPLIMENTS

WE ARE COFFEE
AUCKLAND
EAST CAPE
WELLINGTON
SUPREME
Var 16.16 E
Var 16.24 E
The Traps

COFFEE
SUPREME

ONE

3 KG

ROASTED DAILY.
Coffee
SUPREME
1930

1 KG

FROM:

Shop online

DATE:

KILO

COFFEE SUPREME

BOXER BLEND

CAFE LOCATOR

OPEN COFFEE supreme

Le Marché Cafe

1700 SW 2nd Ave, Miami, FL 33129 USA

Design：Jiani Lu

Le Marché Cafe is a gourmet neighborhood café located in Miami. The brand emblem is a customized logotype featuring a medium weight sans-serif construction paired with blunt serifs. The color palette features a combination of brown and red-orange, to stimulate diners' appetite.

Kuppa Roastery & Café

Commercenter Bldg., 31st St. Cor., 4th Ave., Bonifacio Global City, 1600 Taguig City, Philippines

Studio：Serious Studio

Design：Tintin Lontoc, Deane Miguel, Lester Cruz, Claudine Santos

Kuppa came out as a coffee shop deeply influenced by the third wave of coffee which advocated artisanal coffee. Being one of the first to stand up for this idea, Kuppa wanted to revitalize their brand by reinforcing the exquisite elements of coffee culture, including coffee roaster, tea cup and saucer, latte art and so forth.

Coffee'n'Roll

Komsomolskaya ulitsa, 88, Oryol, Orlovskaya oblast', Russia

Design : Dmitry Neal

Coffee'n'Roll is a company that serves and delivers Japanese food. The packaging highlights a mix of colorful geometric shapes. Circles, diagonal stripes, wavy line were simplified to the maximum with the reference to the main products and ingredients: circles and diagonal stripes represent the salmon fish whereas wavy lines symbolize the sea.

Collected Coffee

Studio : Cumba Co

Design : Kutan Ural

Collected Coffee is a new online-only, high-end, subscription-based retailer that provides distinct beans and roast delivered fresh to subscribers' doorsteps every month. To appeal to sophisticated coffee enthusiasts, the brand identity uses a royal blue as the main color to convey the brand's dedication to exquisite taste.

Recipe

BREWER	Hario V60
GRIND	Medium (19 on Baratza Encore/ Virtuoso/Preciso, 6.75 on EK43)
RATIO	23g coffee 391g water
WATER TEMP	200°F
BREW TIME	4:00
YIELD	350g
TDS	1.35
EXTRACTION	21.34%

Method

1 Add coffee to the rinsed filter and gently shake the V60 to settle the coffee bed.

2 Pour 50g of water over the grounds, saturating the bed. Start your timer.

3 Stir the bed so that all grounds are evenly wet. Once the bed is stirred, let sit until the timer reads 30 seconds.

4 At 30 seconds, pour 100g of water. Pour starting from the center and circle outwards. Once you reach the edge, pour once down the filter to wash any rising grounds back into the brew.

5 Wait until the bed is nearly exposed, then pour another 100g. Repeat until all the water has been added (the last pulse will be 41g larger).

6 When there are no more drips, the brew is complete. Stir coffee and enjoy.

Collected Coffee

Finca La Fortuna
Roasted by
The Barn

06 / 2016

Thank you!

Collected Coffee

Your passport to the world's coffee

CODE

$7 off your order   enjoycollected

collectedcoffee.com
@collectedcoffee

Collected Coffee

Roasted by
The Barn
Berlin, Germany

Finca La Fortuna

Collected Coffee

A collection of the world's best coffee

LYNETTE LEE   617 230 2980
lynette @
collectedcoffee.com

Finca La Fortuna
Huila, Colombia

An estate of just two hectares, Finca La Fortuna lies on a mountainside in Tarqui, a region of Huila, Colombia. Tarqui has not traditionally been popular with coffee farmers as its undulating topography makes crop growth difficult. True to its name, Finca La Fortuna has the good fortune of being seated in a valley with a favorable microclimate, where a gentle wind dries the coffee consistently and evenly.

Neit Guarnizo, owner of Finca La Fortuna, takes part in the Premium Project, an initiative that has enabled him to grow his coffee in a conscious and sustainable way. Each of Finca La Fortuna's coffee cherries is picked and sorted for ripeness. After being washed, the coffee dries in small batches inside the farm's parabolic dryers.

This Caturra from Finca La Fortuna scored a well-deserved 90 points. From the minerality of the soil to the high altitude and ideal climate, every aspect of Finca La Fortuna's growth and harvesting has contributed to its nuanced, complex flavor.

The Barn
Berlin, Germany

In the six years since its inception, The Barn has earned a reputation as one of the most admired coffee institutions in the world. With two locations in Berlin, a café and a café-roastery, The Barn is the project of Ralf Rüller, a financier turned roaster, and is known for its purist approach and pursuit of excellence.

Each season, The Barn sources fresh, single-origin coffees and roasts to showcase their unique flavor profiles. This is the first time The Barn has procured coffee from Finca La Fortuna, and Ralf will visit the estate this fall as part of an ongoing effort to engage directly with farmers.

Finca La Fortuna is unlike any other Colombian coffee, and in featuring this unusual estate, The Barn continues to exceed expectations. In addition, The Barn began projects this year analyzing how water quality across eight countries and experimenting with a custom build Probat UG-22 roaster. From sourcing to execution, The Barn seeks to constantly innovate.

Collected Coffee
New York, United States

Finca La Fortuna's intense aroma of sweet, dark stone fruit surpassed all other coffees on the cupping table. Reminiscent of ripe plums bursting at their skins, the coffee is more akin to its East African counterparts than any Colombian in recent memory.

Finca La Fortuna is dense, and its roast profile, while light, is fully developed. This versatile coffee embraces a higher extraction and shines on any brew method. We recommend increasing the amount of water to boost extraction; this allows for more clarity in the cup while giving the expansive flavors room to breathe.

We like Finca La Fortuna best as a V60 brewed at a coffee to water ratio of 1:17, and at a lower strength of 1.35 TDS. We chose a V60 to naturally accentuate the coffee's brighter characteristics. Pour in pulses to lengthen the contact time, but use slightly cooler water at 200°F to control the rate of extraction. As the coffee cools, its blackberry notes give way to brown sugar sweetness.

Peat Me

Nizhniy Susalnyy Street, 5c1, Moscow, Russia 105064

Studio : YellowBrand

Design : Evgeny Shiskarev

Peat Me is a team of peculiar people who believe in the spirit of unicorn. The studio developed a logo of unicorn with a fork instead of a horn. The packaging took inspiration from the street culture of Moscow where young people wearing sneakers and riding skateboard are everywhere.

Square One
Coffee Roasters

249 S. 13th St. Philadelphia, PA 19107, USA

Studio : Pop & Pac

Square One Coffee Roasters is a new coffee roasting company establishing its name in Melbourne's inner south-east. The design takes inspiration from the coffee bean's African and Central American origins, the coffee roasting process and the distinctively unique flavor characteristics in their respective brews. Different colors are used for the packaging to show the types of coffee: red for the Espresso blend, blue for single origin and green for filter.

Combi Coffee

Studio : 327 Creative Studio

Design : Mafalda Portal, Inês Vieira, Ana Noversa

Combi Coffee reflects the current trend of mobile food/beverage trucks in Porto, Portugal. The color palette of the truck—black, white and olive green—were manually painted. The geometrical icon set of cups is the communication basis developed to present the ingredients used in the different varieties of Combi coffee.

Micio Caffè

No. 60, Section 3, Nuzhong Road, Yilan City, Yilan County, Taiwan 260

Studio : Transform Design

"Micio" is an Italian word for kitten. The brand name was inspired by a kitten of tenacious vitality. The founders of Micio Caffè wanted to pass on its spirit and made it the core values of the brand. Therefore, the studio took the idea from the image of cats and developed the logo with the use of geometrical shapes, showing a sense of tenderness and purity.

Nord Coffee Roastery

Studio : Cumba Co

Design : Kutan Ural

Nord Coffee Roastery is a brand emerging along with the third wave of coffee. To make the brand stand out in the crowd, the studio got inspired by the Nordic style suggested by the brand name. To start with, the logo was designed to be flat and minimalistic. The packaging was designed with simple geometrical elements: circle, line, and dot. The concentric circles present the most well-known symbol of the Nordic area: the polar lights.

MOK

Rue Antoine Dansaert 196, 1000 Brussels, Belgium

Design : Matthias Deckx

MOK Specialty Coffee Roastery & Bar is a fast growing specialty coffee roastery in Belgium. The logo consists of an abstract monogram which can be used separately as a pattern for promotional material. The MOK logo can be dissected into three primary shapes, indicating respectively the different types of coffee: Espresso, Filter and Omni roast. Four colors are used to further emphasize the single-origin and blend coffee types.

 MOK
Specialty Coffee
Roastery & Bar

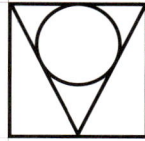 MOK
Specialty Coffee
Roastery & Bar

Café Frida

15 Rue des Forges, Trois-Rivières G9A 4X6, Canada

Design : Marie-Michelle Dupuis, Pier-Luc Cossette

Frida Khalo is one of the most iconic artists of the 20th century, known as not only a genius painter, but also a hero to indigenous Mexicans and feminists around the world. The brand identity paid tribute to her recognizable flower-filled paintings and Mexican traditions. The floral pattern was hand painted to convey a real yet rough feel.

café
FRIDA

HUEVOS RANCHEROS 7.⁰⁰
oeufs, tortillas & garnitures

CROQUE MADAME 8.⁵⁰
au cheddar & jambon + salade

2 OEUFS 6.⁵⁰
bacon fumé artisanal & pain grillé

POMMES DE TERRE 4.⁰⁰
selon l'humeur du chef

QUICHE 9.⁵⁰
légumes et fromage + salade

① commandez à la caisse
② recevez votre boisson au comptoir
③ attendez votre repas à la table

Coffee & Co.

Tallink Silja Line cruise ship

Studio : Bond

Design : Jesper Bange, James Zambra

Coffee & Co. is a new cafeteria project on a Tallink Silja Line cruise ship offering freshly prepared savory and sweet snacks. The aim of the project was to create a friendly and straight forward identity, comfortable for all the passengers on board. The script typography underlines a casual feeling and communicates the selection of offered products.

The Niteowl Cafe

250 Chulia Street, Penang Island, Malaysia

Design : ZiYu Ooi

Niteowl is a modern late-night cafe situated amidst the vibrant Penang's old street, aiming to cater the city's night owls who crave for midnight munchies. The logo was designed to be a monogram of the letters of the brand name, and the little owl placed in the center of the logo added the final touch to the whole. The cyan color was used to meet with the cafe's positioning as a late-night hangout place.

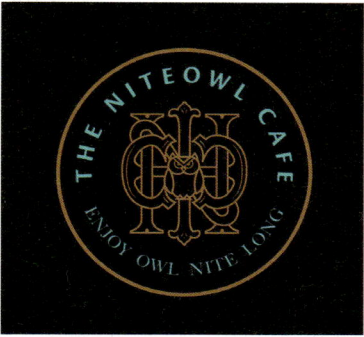

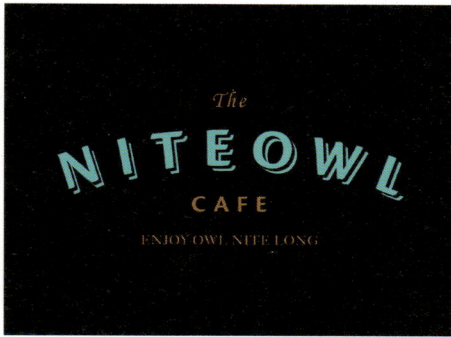

Yeahnot

Nezalezhnosti embankment, 4-8, Uzhhorod, Ukraine

Designer: Marina Mescaline

Photographer: Mihail Melnichenko

Yeahnot terrace is a cafe that serves breakfast and brunch and transforms into a cocktail bar in the evening. The English words "yeah" and "not" together sound like the Ukrainian word "yenot" which means "racoon". The opposition between the two words leads to the main concept: lazy breakfast in the morning and wild cocktail party with DJs in the evening. The Memphis style visual identity is based on the lightness of terrace design and the diverse choices of food and cocktail.

breakfast / brunch
salads
snacks
main
soup
pasta
drinks
coffee

yeah
not

Bronuts

3 - 100 King Street, Winnipeg MB Canada

Studio：One Plus One Design

Designer：Tyler Thiessen, Jessie Thiessen

Bronuts is a coffee shop located in the Exchange District in Winnipeg, Canada, which means a large number of footfall. Starting from the brand name, which is a combination of "bro" and "donuts", a smile and the shape of a donut have been further developed into visual elements of the logo. Running with this connotation, the studio engineered a crisp brand identity with a chic personality. The exterior and interior signage, menu design, individual and group donuts packaging were all consistently designed for engaging customer experience.

INTERIOR

P100~205

Creating the Coffee Shop Brand Experience

John Barnett, Anna Burles (JB | AB Design)

JB | AB Design is an international design studio based in London. John Barnett and Anna Burles have worked extensively on creating coffee shop environments within the UK, Russia and China. The studio takes a multidisciplinary approach combining disciplines from architecture, branding, graphics, exhibition design through to interior design and production.

Designing a coffee shop isn't just about getting the right look. Or serving the best coffee. It's about creating an experience which not only shouts about the amazingness of your coffee, and how that makes people feel good, but also an experience which gives a double-shot boost to your brand.

We design coffee shops in different parts of the world for clients who roast and grind and brew really great coffee. We are also serious coffee drinkers, which handily makes us a target consumer for the brands we work for. The challenge for our clients is that we, like coffee lovers everywhere, are increasingly spoiled for choice.

It's a crowded marketplace for sure, with an ever-growing breed of artisan coffee brands opening up shop in our towns and cities. So what makes us (or you) choose one shop over the others? And how can we as designers use our professional and personal insight to help you as a client stand out in a way which makes consumers stay loyal to you?

Through our work in the coffee industry, we sometimes find clients feeling perplexed about how to approach the design of their shops in terms of identifying the most important elements to get right. We usually advise taking a step back to look at the business as a whole, to see what the new venue needs to deliver on all fronts.

A successful coffee shop integrates everything the brand represents into a three-dimensional space—not just a cool interior, but great customer service, a great product, smart and efficient operations and a powerful identity brought to life through branding and innovative graphics. Everything works together to create something even bigger. All the parts have to work in sync, otherwise the cracks will start to show and the business suffers.

1. Share the same creative & business goals

The Holy Grail for designer and client has to be the same from the outset. To design something different, which cuts through the competition, the interior design should deliver not only an exciting visual experience, but one which works to drive foot traffic and make money for the brand. If your designer is only interested in creating the hottest new look in town, run for the hills.

2. Bring the customer to the center stage

The coffee shop experience should always be built around the customer and the design tailored to fit him or her, culturally, socially and geographically, like a glove. Today's consumers are savvy and warm to brands which mirror their view of themselves in the world, responding less and less to identikit design. So it follows that coffee shops in a chain shouldn't be clones of each other, but tailored to fit the space you've chosen. Adding a local twist can make all the difference to making the consumer feel that the shop has been designed thoughtfully for him or her.

3. Get the customer journey right and the rest will follow

Understanding how customers will interact with the space is the key. From what they see when they approach the shop from across the street to how they move through the space. What they see at any given point will drive the decisions they make. We always put ourselves in the place of the customer, analyzing the way different types of customers might make decisions about the brand in and out of the shop. These decisions drive the interior design, spatial arrangements, bar configuration, graphic communications and customer service. Exploring this helps us work with the brand to talk to the customer through the design of the shop at the exact point where they make their decision.

4. Make sure design and operations are integrated

If you want to create an amazing interior display of coffee beans or coffee bags, make sure you also put in place some strict visual merchandising rules to maintain the display, or it will fall apart, become messy.

The coffee shop is the biggest and one of the most expensive marketing tools a business has and it should be used for maximum effect. The store design is like a silent barista, talking to the customer in discreet ways, in a tone that makes them warm to your brand and love what you do.

6 tips for creating an exciting environment:

1. The shop is a stage

Showcase your baristas'skills: all the care and attention that goes into preparing the perfect cup. This is the key to educating the customer about specialty coffee. Every point in the customer journey should be focused on spotlighting the barista and the theatre of making coffee. Help people understand the craft of great coffee and they will be encouraged to try new things. The design and spatial planning of the whole environment needs to focus on this.

2. Customers eat with their eyes

The way to a person's stomach is through his or her eyes. Which is why mouth-watering food and drink display and photography are significant to the commercial success of the menu. Creating sumptuous imagery will stimulate the perception of taste, aroma and appeal.

3. Say it like you mean it

Graphic communication shouldn't just be confined to the menu. The whole shop is a canvas for imagery and messaging that forms the basis of a conversation with your customers. Graphics can be updated and changed inexpensively, keeping the brand fresh and relevant. Graphics need to say something inspiring, not just look pretty. Use graphics to showcase your baristas'skills, your specialty coffee and the great taste of your food. Customers can sometimes feel overwhelmed by too many choices, so using graphics to tell a visual story can help them navigate the options more easily.

Travelers Coffee

4. See it, like it, buy it

The single most important principle we adopt when we're designing is "See it, Like it, Buy it." Great visual merchandising sells products. Easy to understand, accessible displays, attractive, persuasive point of sale and clear pricing at every customer decision point (not just at the bar) will increase revenue.

5. Creating ambience

Never underestimate the power of great lighting. It will transform the environment, creating the right mood and focus exactly where you want the customer's eye to land. Yet it is one of the elements so often overlooked and under-budgeted.

6. Gather round the table

Customers know exactly what they want from their individual coffee moments, and the environment needs to give it to them, offering different reasons to visit whatever the occasion, time pressure or mood. Flexible design and clever seating arrangements will create special solitary spaces for those who seek them, as well as buzzy zones where people can enjoy socializing with friends.

Commercial design has two functions: to give pleasure and to sell. Focusing our work on both of these at every stage of the design process creates real value for customers and owners. We also tend to get involved in every detail of the coffee shops we're designing. Not only concepting the space itself but every element of the brand experience, helping design everything from the architecture to the interior look and feel, as well as how the brand identity comes to life in the space, the graphics on the walls and menu boards, even down to the uniforms. We find this holistic approach works particularly well to make sure good design becomes good business.

The Budapest Café

Dongcheng International No.7- 8, Chenghua District, Chengdu, Sichuan Province, China

Studio : Biasol

© James Morgan

Inspired by filmmaker Wes Anderson's distinctive visual style and Melbourne's café culture, the studio's fresh and modern interpretation of café is defined by design, materiality and brand. Much like Anderson's mythical Budapest Hotel, the Budapest Café is designed to offer an experience that detaches patrons from the hustle and bustle of everyday life. The brief is to create an international hospitality experience, and a space that would appeal to social media-savvy females who enjoy café culture. It is also designed to be fun, and the layers, elevations and surprising design features encourage customers to explore and physically engage with the space.

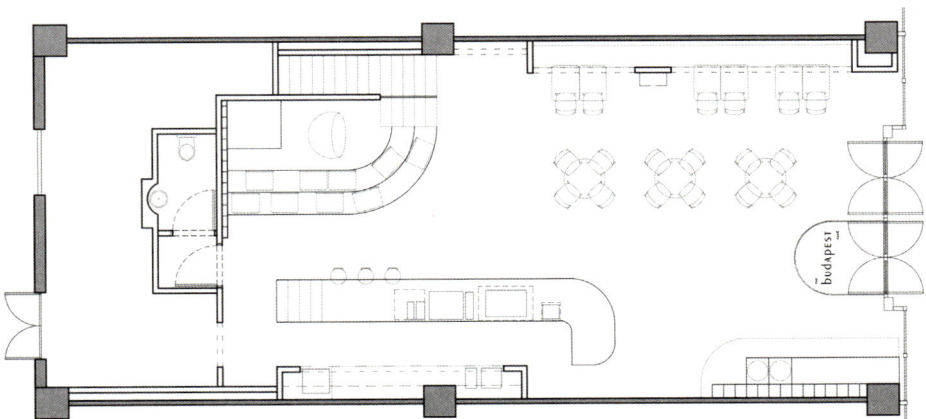

A mezzanine level provides a view from above, one of Anderson's signature perspectives.

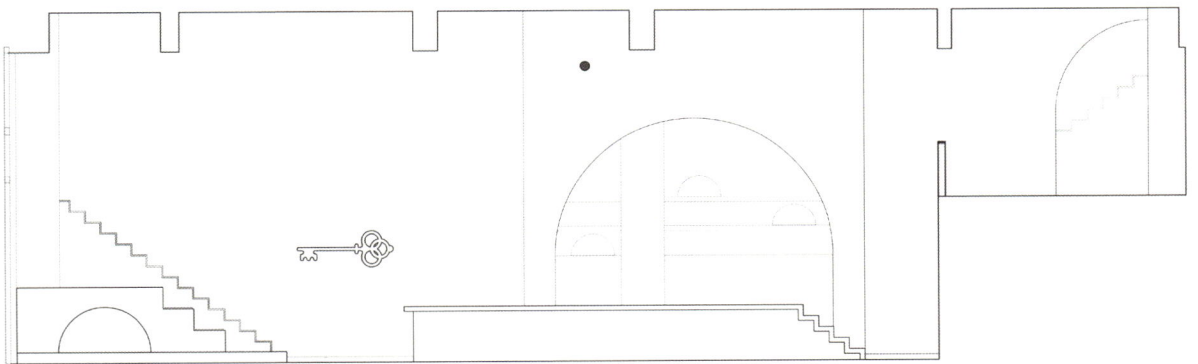

A pink ball pool, neon signage and original Eero Aarnio Bubble chair inspire playfulness.

Symmetrical arches frame recessed seating and shelving.

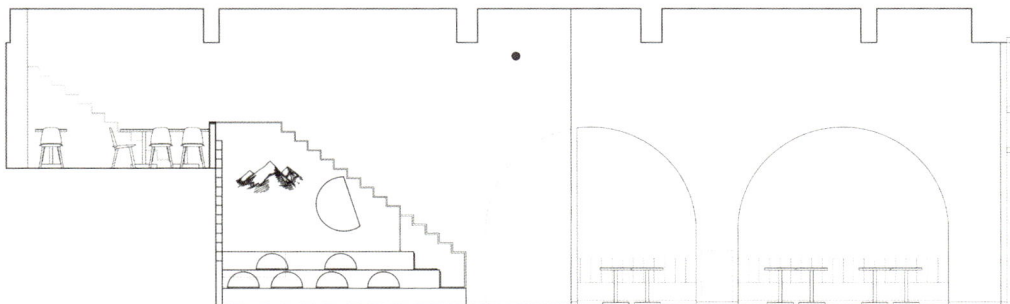

The bathrooms surprise with speckled pink terrazzo to complement and contrast with the nostalgic-green hues of the café.

Daily

33 Rishelievska str.Odessa, Ukraine

Studio : Sivak+Partners

Design : Maksym Luriichuk, Dmitriy Sivak, Cyrill Verbych

Daily is a place you can visit on a daily basis. It is not just a coffee shop, but also kind of an urban space offering social events where inspiring speeches are shared with guests. The café has two separate zones: one is a spacious room with a counter, a seating area and plenty of lighting. The dimmable wall lights create a warm and cozy atmosphere throughout the day. The suspended lamps over the counter and the main furniture were custom made; the other has a very special intimate atmosphere where you can enjoy some quiet time with a book and a cup of coffee, with friends, or with your date.

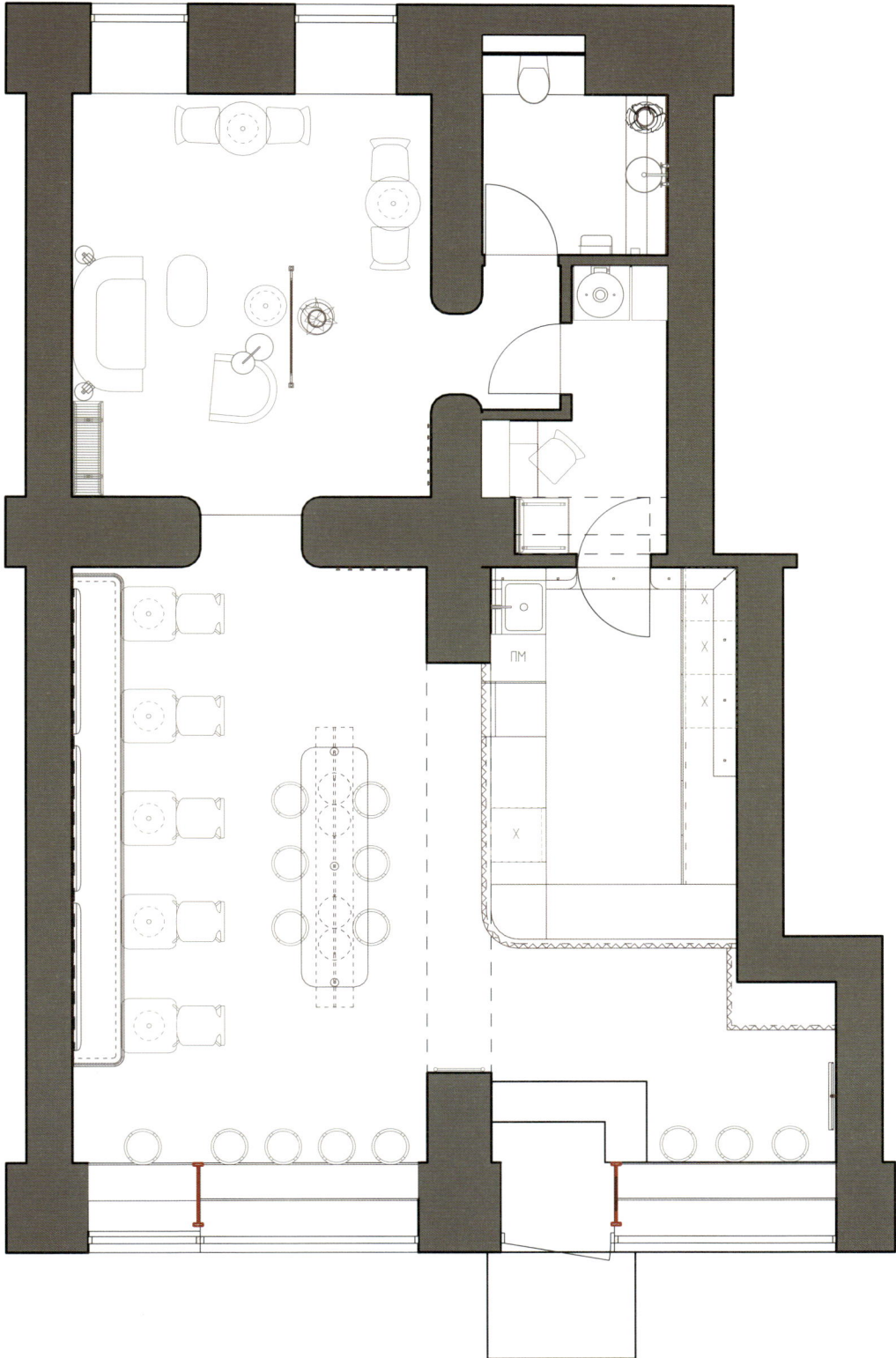

КОФЕ
ЭСПРЕССО   40
ФИЛЬТР КОФЕ   40
КАПУЧИНО   45
ЛАТТЕ   45
ФЛЕТ УАЙТ   50
РАФ   60

ХОЛОДНЫЕ НАПИТКИ
АЙС МАТЧА ЛАТТЕ   90
КАСКАРА ФИЗ   50
ЛИМОНАД   65

КОЛД БРЮ
ЧЕРНЫЙ   55
МОЛОКО   65
ТОНИК
ФРЕШ
АВТОРСКИЙ

ГОРЯЧИЕ НАПИТКИ
КАКАО
МАТЧА   75
МАТЧА ЛАТТЕ   80
ЧАЙ   45
КАСКАРА   50

АЛЬТЕРНАТИВА
V60   55
ЭСПРЕСС   55

Pirogi

Pies and Friends, 20A Pushkinska St, Kyiv, Ukraine

Studio : Balbek Bureau

Design : Slava Balbek, Yevheniia Dubrovskaya

© Yevhenii Avramenko

Pirogi is a modern cozy bakery café located in the historic district of Kyiv city center. The main task of the architectural team was to make inviting homelike vibes for every guest. The café is specialized in homemade sweet pies which are baked right in front of the guests. To focus the guests' attention on the specialty, three large wood tables are integrated in the center of the first hall. They harmoniously match the natural granite on the floor that smoothly continues up the walls. The second hall offers larger space for seating. Several bright color accents are introduced in the interior: a blue sofa in the recessed window, colorful panels on the wall and a bright burgundy restroom.

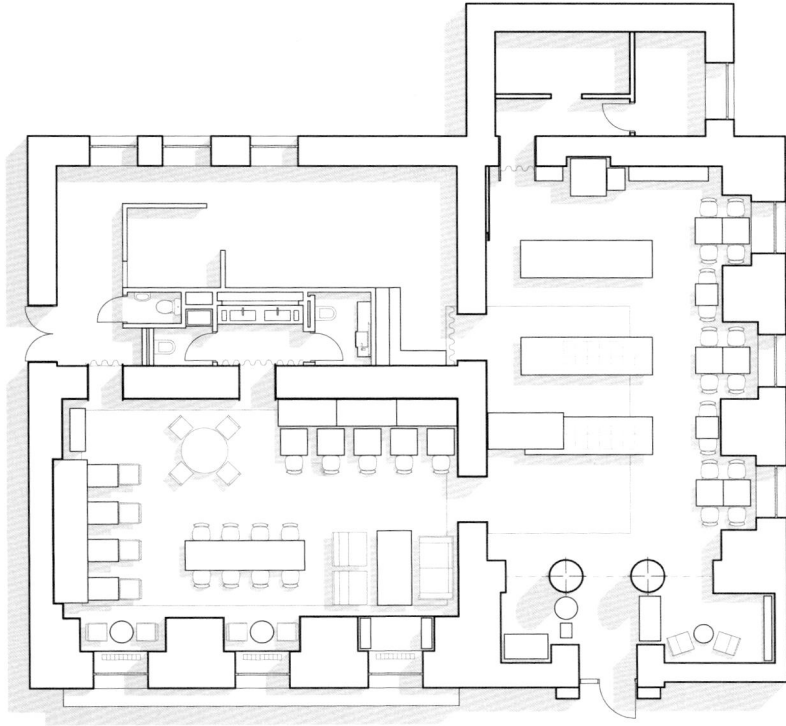

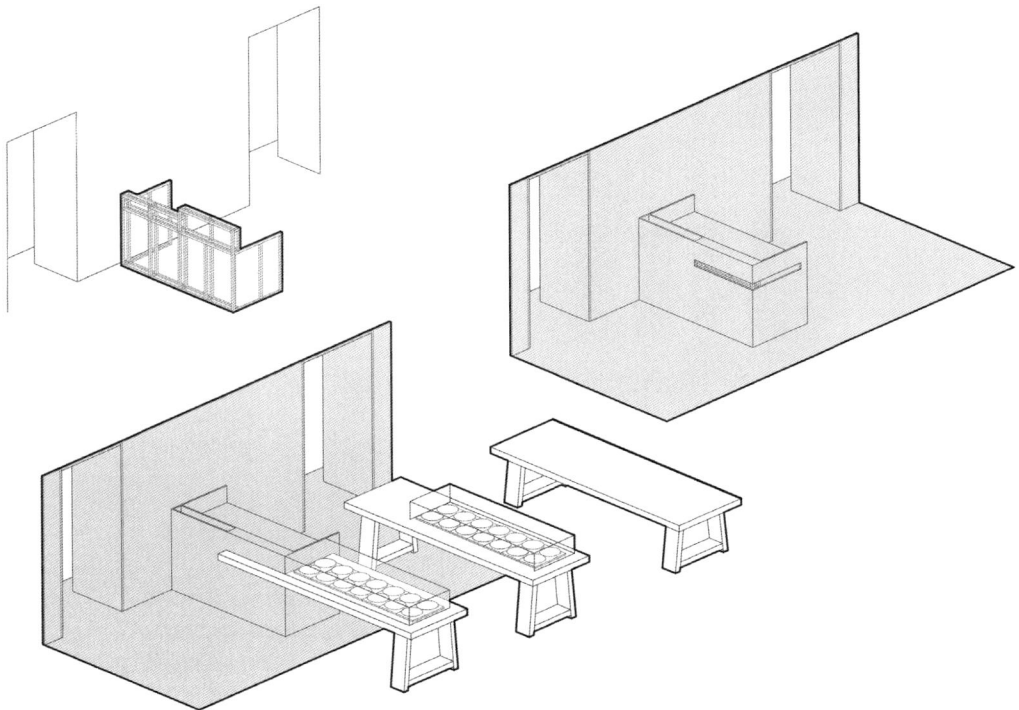

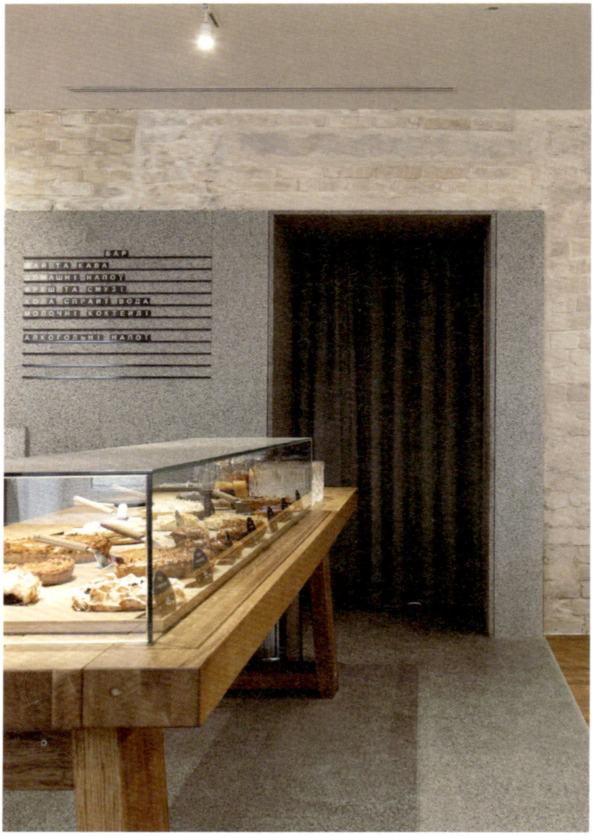
БАР
МОЛОЧНІ КОКТЕЙЛІ
АЛКОГОЛЬНІ НАПОЇ

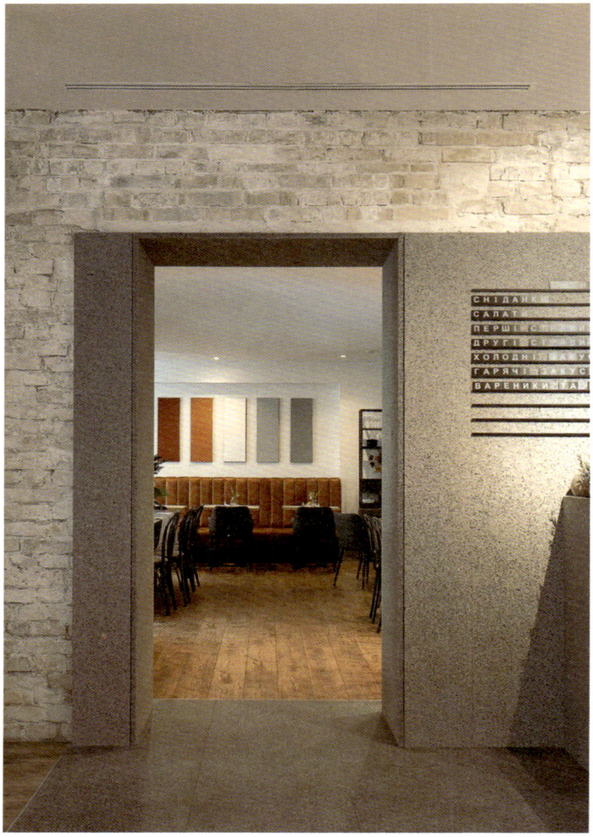

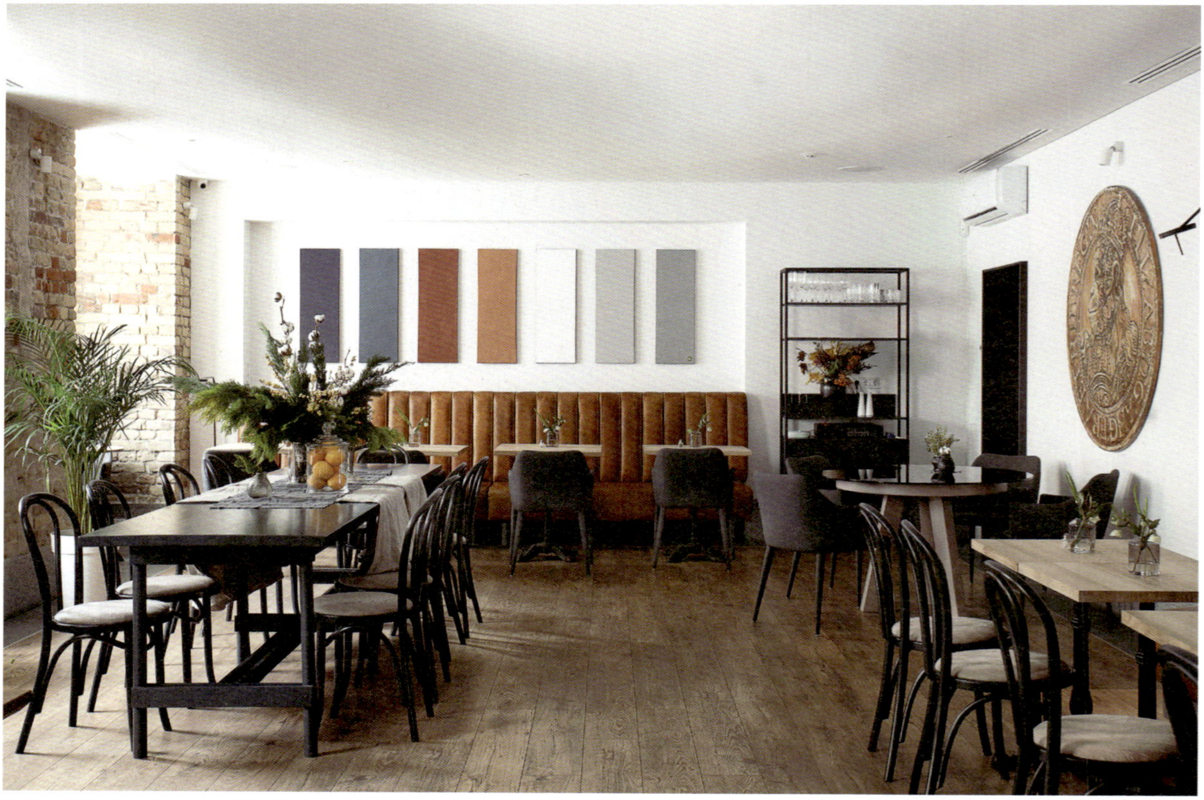

Skurator Coffee Kazan

Baumana 9, Kazan, Russia

Studio：Maket Interior

Design：Ostroukhov Konstantin

© Georgy Trushkin

The coffeehouse is located in a pedestrian zone in the center of Kazan. It is decorated in loft style emphasized by hanging lights and greenery and neon signs, and most basic materials are used: metal, concrete, and wood. An area of 225m2 have been divided into three zones—bar, seating area, and workshop area. The bar area is highlighted with a bar counter made of blue glass blocks with backlight; the seating area consists of separate tables, a large karagach wood table, and two vintage leather sofas; the workshop area has been arranged snuggly in the center, separated by partitions made of metal and glass.

Альтернативное меню:
V 60 170
Аэропресс 170
Сифон 170
Колд брю 170
Нитро 150

Открытые мероприятия в августе:
Дегустация ягод 11.08. 17:00
Правила каппинга 18.08. 17:00
Чемпионат по каптестингу 25.08. 17:00
Уголок потребителя
Skuratov coffee
1 место

Skuratov Coffee Moscow

Mira 26/1, Moscow, Russia

Studio : Maket Interior

Design : Ostroukhov Konstantin

© Leonid Syomov

Situated next to the Botanical Garden of Moscow University, the café is settled in a historical district which led to the classic style of its interior. Rather than adopting the traditional classic style, the designer employed elements of hotels and motels of the 1930s-50s, such as brass, marble and wood. The ball-shaped lighting and the blue color for the wall took reference from the round lamps and the blue-green window shades outside the building. For an area as small as 28m², the designer opted for a long bar table set along the length of the window. The most eye-catching decoration is a neon sign of the outline map of Omsk region where Skuratov Coffee was created.

PORTLAND
NEW YORK
MOSCOW
KAZAN
OMSK CITY
MENU
КЛАССИКА
ЧЕРНЫЙ КОФЕ
SKURATOV TECHNOLOGY
SWEET & SEASON
КОФЕ
НЕ КОФЕ
SKURATOV
50% СКИДКА
НА ВСЮ ЕДУ
В ХОЛОДИЛЬНИКЕ
ВО ВСЕХ КОФЕЙНЯХ

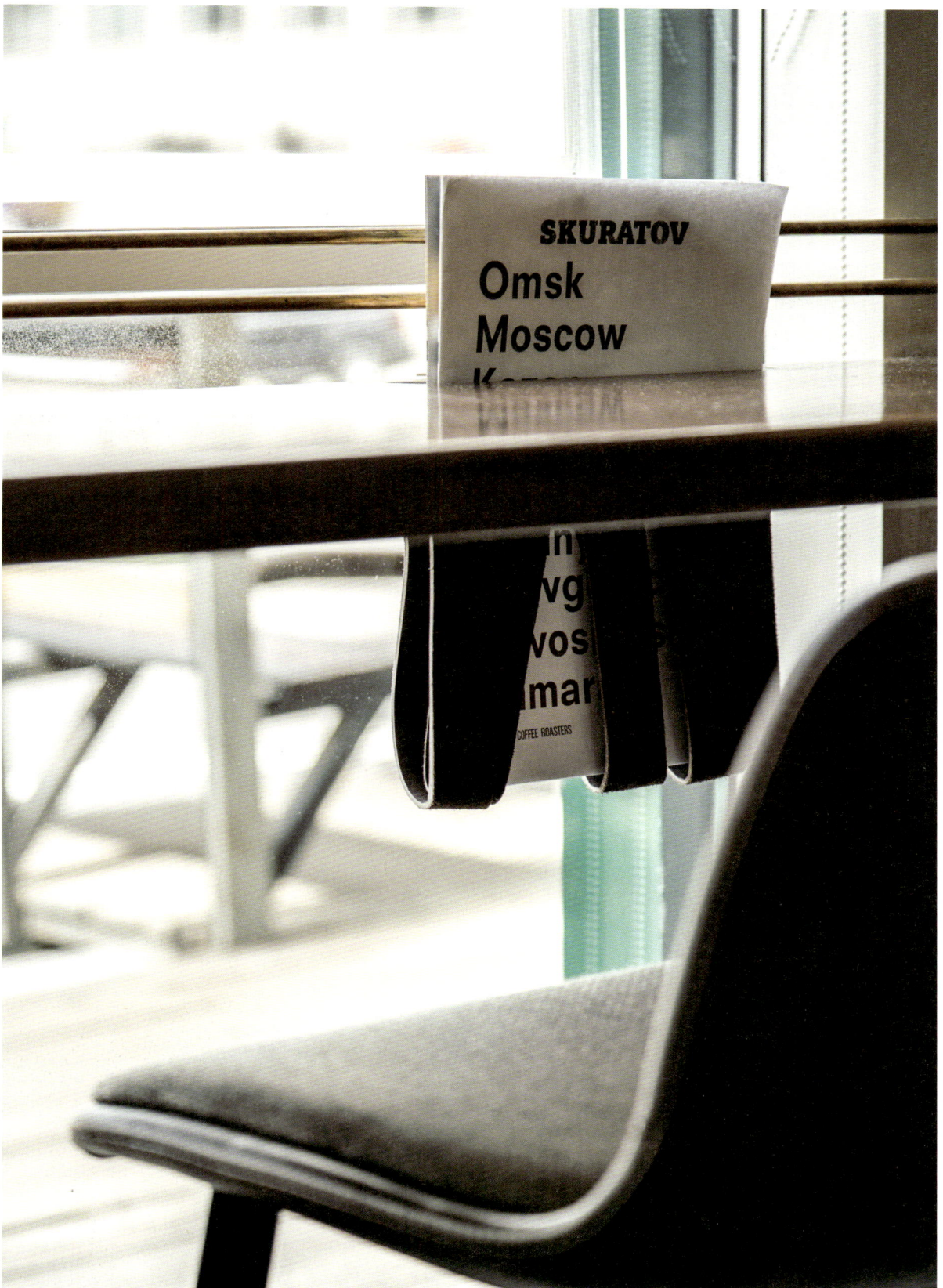

Shan Café

Jing Yuan Arts Center, 3 Guangqu Rd., Changyang District, Beijing, China

Studio : Robot3 Design

Design : Fei Pan, Zhibang Shao, Xiaohan Li

© Xixun Deng

The first and second floors of the office building needed to be renovated into a café where customers can stay and communicate freely. Because the first Shan café is located at the foot of the Fragrant Hills of Beijing, this café needs to maintain a consistent image related to hills as well.

1F

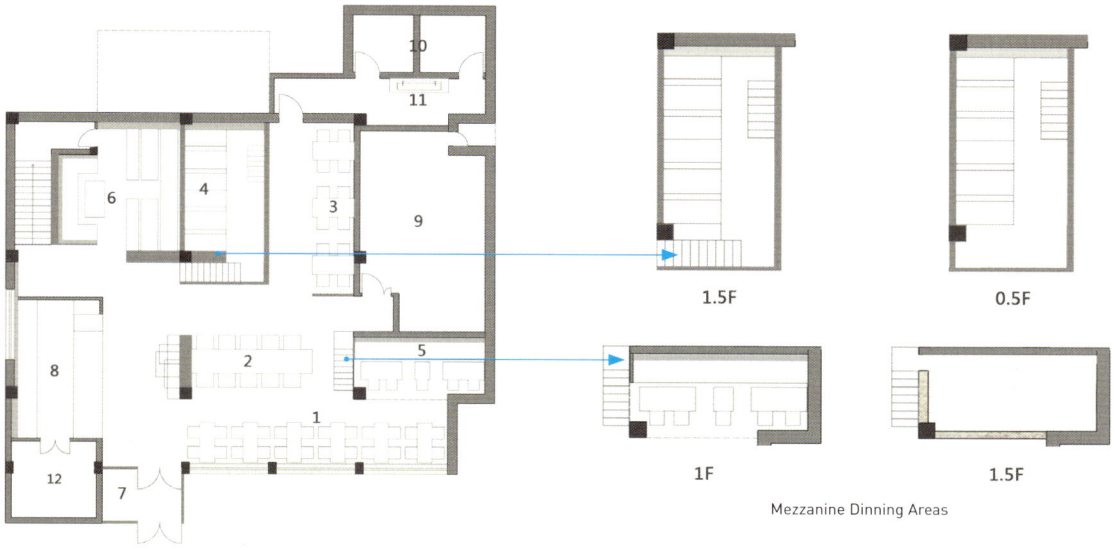

1.5F

0.5F

1F

1.5F

Mezzanine Dinning Areas

1~6. Dinning Area 1~6, 7. Vestibule, 8. Cashier, 9. Kitchen, 10. Restroom, 11. Washbasin, 12. Storage Room

Sectional View A

Sectional View B

The team dug down one meter at the center of the space so that there is enough space to build a mezzanine.

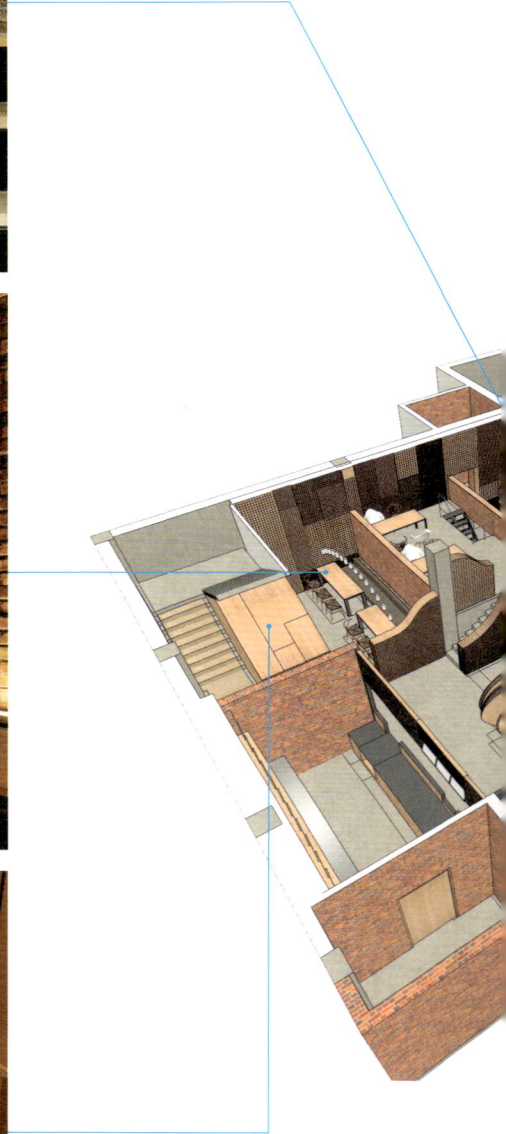

Beside the stairs leading to the upper floor, a small cabin is built to contain a large group of customers.

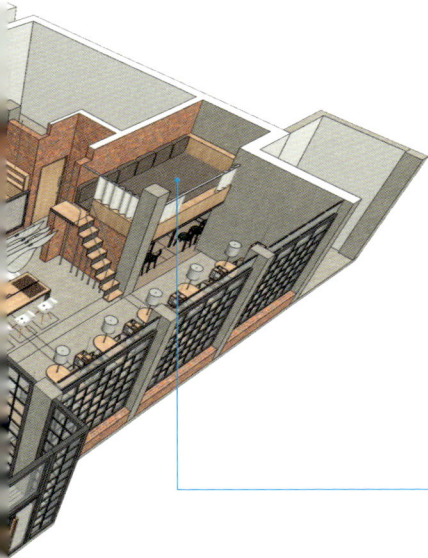

The height of the mezzanine is only big enough for customers to sit or lie down, but it is perfect for private chatting.

2F

13~17 Private Dining Room 1~5, 18 Office, 19 VIP Private Dining Room, 20 Seats, 21 Restroom, 22 Washbasin, 23 Terrace

Dogs & Tails

19 Shota Rustaveli St, Kyiv, Ukraine

Studio : Makhno Studio

Design : Sergey Makhno

© Andrey Bezuglov

Concrete, black-painted iron and wood are the main materials used for the interior. The industrial atmosphere is reinforced by the rigid angular geometry of structural and decorative elements, as well as the harsh light emanating from the custom designed tubular neon lights hanging over the bar. The turquoise ceiling of the main bar area brightens the interior, balancing the strong industrial feel.

Truth Coffee

36 Buitenkant St, Cape Town City Centre, Cape Town, 8000 South Africa

Design : Haldane Martin

Haldane Martin was invited to create interior design as well as all bespoke furniture and fittings for Truth Coffee. The designer came up with the idea of steampunk which was taken as an appropriate conceptual reference, as the café's coffee roasters and espresso machines display elements of the romantic, steam-powered technology. Steampunk's obsession with details and sensual aesthetics also captured the essence of Truth Coffee's philosophy: roast coffee properly.

As the kingpin for the space, the huge, fully functioning vintage roaster was positioned at the center of the space and a circular steel shelving structure was placed surrounding it, reminiscent of the Victorian gas works.

Purpose-designed overstuffed, leather and steel chairs, bar stools and copper-clad tables create a formal raised dining area in front of the bar.

A series of five horseshoe-shaped, deep buttoned, high backed banquet seats runs down along the right-hand wall of the space. Each private banquet seat surrounds a long, narrow, profile-cut steel table.

The over-scaled cog teeth on the edges of the table tops encourage groups of patrons to share tables to facilitate larger informal gatherings.

Aschan Café Jugend

Pohjoisesplanadi 19, Helsinki 00100, Finland

Studio : Bond

Design : Aleksi Hautamaki, Tuomas Hautamaki

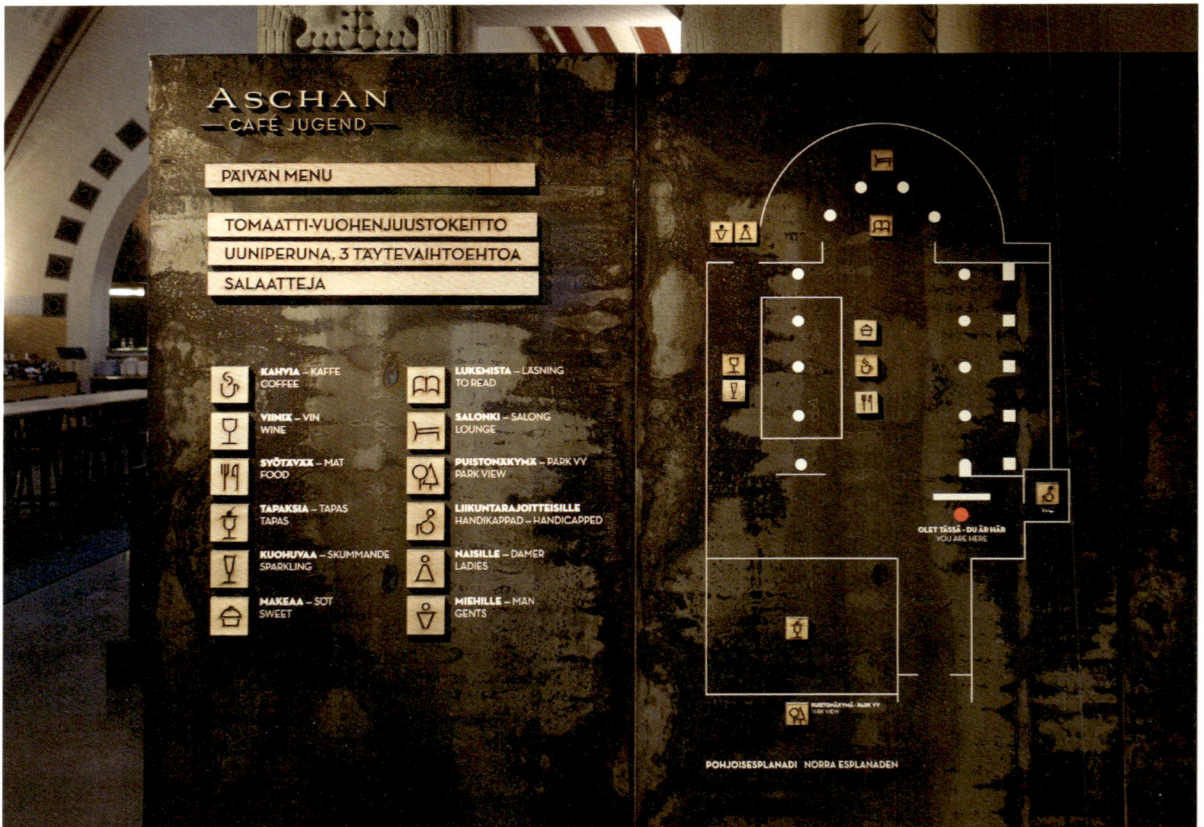

The Jugend Hall in the Uschakoff Building was originally opened in 1904 as a banking hall. As it is an architectural heritage, the interior design had to just float on the floor. The space consists of a central bank hall with lower aisles on both sides and a large six-meter high dome at the rear end.

In the middle of the central hall, the designers created an area with five-meter long tables, which allows for a more social atmosphere. Towards both sides and the back, the atmosphere gets more intimate as there is a raised seating area with soft flooring and dim lighting. The floor there was raised to get variation in the room height and to better the proportions of the vast, open space. The use of carpets underneath the furniture was essential in keeping the acoustics down as there is a lot of echo. The oiled oak was combined with blackened metal and dark gray fabrics.

Underneath the dome there is a magazine library with the latest issues on culture, design and art. The lighting towers in front of the columns house up-lighters.

The wall lights were replaced by indirect lighting and table lights bring the scale down. Between the columns seating is arranged in booths.

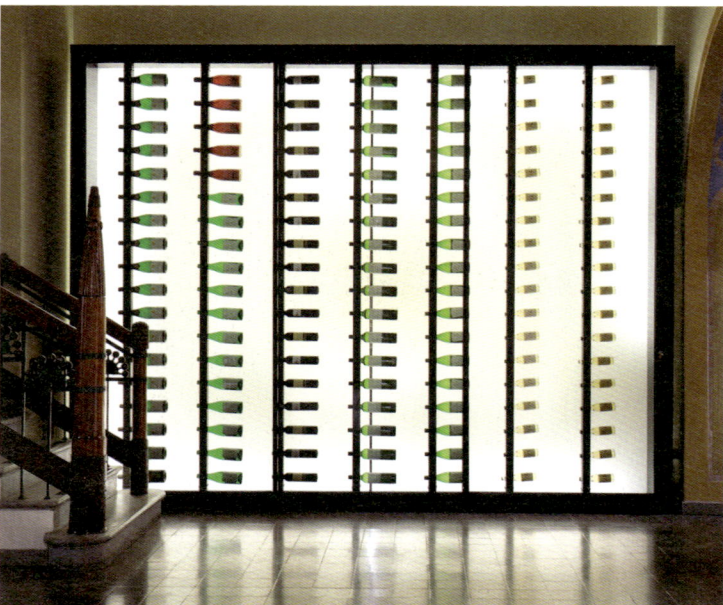

Dishoom

12 Upper St. Martin's Lane, London WC2H 9FB, UK

Studio : AfroditiKrassa

Design : Afroditi Krassa

© Sim Canetty-Clarke

The old Irani cafés in South Asia opened last century by Zoroastrian Irani immigrants was once popular in the 1960s and have almost all disappeared now. The branch store of Dishoom, a 5,000 square feet venue, is an unexpected contemporary interpretation of a traditional Irani café. Drawing on Bombay's rich pop culture—street stalls and down-to-earth eateries—the interior combines elegant, sophisticated and simple lines with the Bombay's art decor in the past, while making reference to the present-day London.

STAIR 3

1:15 Ramp (276mm Rise)

1:12 Ramp (70mm Rise)

Fire Exit Door by Landlord

LIFT 3

Prep Kitchen

1:12 Ramp (94mm Rise)

1800mm Headroom at this point

Corridor

Cold room

1:15 Ramp (270mm Rise)

Dry Store

LIFT 2

Steps

Staff Changing & WC's

Electric Cupboard

High Level Cupboard boxed in over sockets

Bar Store

Bar

LIFT 1

Male Toilets

Privacy Screen Detail TBC

Ambulant Disabled Cubicle as Diagram 21 Part M

Stub Stack with AAV

Ambulant Disabled Cubicle as Diagram 21 Part M

Indicative route of 100mm drain pipe under raised floor

Disabled Platform Lift

Platform Lift Door to open on this face

Disabled WC

Female Toilets

Steps

Steps

Stub Stack with AAV

Restaurant

Banquette Seating

Screen Detail TBC

Banquette Seating

Banquette Seating

Existing Drahning to be opened up to concealed waste pipework

Existing Manhole to remain accessible. Banquette seating to be removable

Drain connection extended through vault to pipwork connection for 2 WC's, set tight to back wall of vaults as possible. Height of pipe as it passes through wall to be maximum 170mm to centre line. Landlord has formed opening through vault wall to facilitate this.

Bottom

Banquette Seating

Water Station

Connections to seating manhole removed and capped to access required

Office

Existing Manhole to remain accessible

157

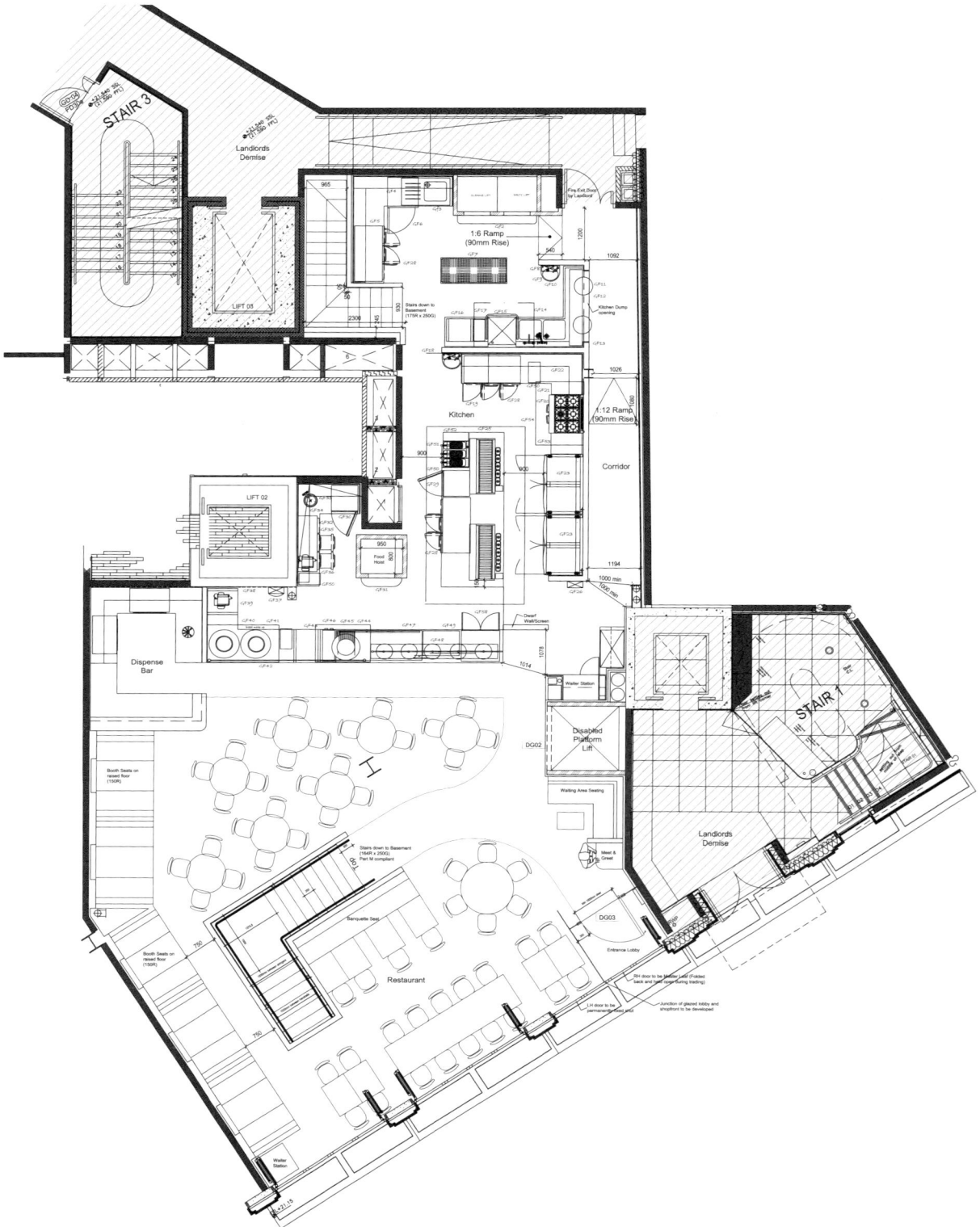

STAIR 3

GO·04
FCD/N

+21,340 SSL
(T.350 PFL)

+21,350 PFL

Landlords
Demise

965

LIFT 03

Stairs down to
Basement
(17SR x 250G)

2300

1:6 Ramp
(90mm Rise)

Fire Exit Door
for Landlord

1300

1092

1026

Kitchen Dump
opening

540

900

LIFT 02

950
Food Hoist

1:12 Ramp
(90mm Rise)

1026

Corridor

Dwarf
Wall/Screen

1194

1000 min

1000 min

1014

1078

Dispense
Bar

Waiter Station

STAIR 1

Booth Seats on
raised floor
(150R)

Disabled
Platform
Lift

DG02

Waiting Area Seating

Meet &
Greet

Landlords
Demise

Stairs down to Basement
(16.4R x 250G)
Part M compliant

Banquette Seat

Restaurant

750

Booth Seats on
raised floor
(150R)

750

DG03

Entrance Lobby

RH door to be held open (Folded
back and held open during trading)

LH door to be
permanently fixed shut

Junction of glazed lobby and
shopfront to be developed

Waiter Station

158

Custom-made checkerboard tiles, oak paneling, white Carrara marble-topped tables and mismatched chairs create a relaxed, democratic café-style space.

Antique mirrors, slowly turning ceiling fans, a lighting scheme that includes bespoke glass orbs and a feature wall of retro portraiture all contribute to a light and airy modern space.

RULES OF THE CAFÉ

NO SMOKING
NO FIGHTING
NO CREDIT
NO FOOD FROM OUTSIDE
NO TALKING LOUD
NO SPITTING
NO BARGAINING
NO CHEATING
NO WATER TO OUTSIDERS
NO MATCHES
NO GAMBLING
NO COMBING HAIR
ALL CASTES WELCOME

Cafe 27

Building 2, 6 Fangyuan Xilu, Chaoyang District, Beijing, 100015 China

Studio: Four O Nine

Design: Andrei Zerebecky, Lukasz Kos

© Hu Yihuai

The project is a retrofit of an existing glass greenhouse structure into a new flagship for the launch of the Cafe 27 brand. The new café was made an inside-out garden pavilion where a number of elements were placed inside a passively controlled greenhouse that connects with its surroundings.

The green wall is an attempt to purify Beijing's polluted air as it makes its way inside. Combined with the terrazzo flooring, it creates a thermal mass that gradually and passively heats the space in the winter. In summer time, the exterior wood trellis shades the glass structure reducing undesirable heat gain.

A massive ceramic bar with pastry display anchors the interior seating arrangement.

The interior and exterior are connected through a series of pivoting doors further blurring the boundary between the indoor and outdoor space of the cafe.

Proti Proudu Bistro

Březinova 22/471, 186 00 Praha 8 – Karlín, Czech Republic

Studio : Mimosa Architekti

© Jakub Skokan, Martin Tuma

Connecting each other through good coffee and delicious food is the main theme of the interior design. Network of wires, stretching from the switches behind the counter to the lights above the tables, represents the connection between staff and guests. Plywood texture of the walls softly coordinates with stone floor pattern and the oak board of the counter and tables. Steel element used in the lamps and chairs preserves a calm black iron character.

Tostado Café Club

Av. Córdoba 1501, Ciudad Autónoma de Buenos Aires, Argentina

Studio : Hitzig Militello Arquitectos

Design : Fernando Hitzig, Leonardo Militello

© Federico Kulekdjian

To recreate the spirit of the traditional Buenos Aires groceries, the studio worked with its most obvious representation: the wooden box for groceries. The floors and walls made of graphite gray calcarean tiles whose surface was polished to enhance the intrinsic qualities of the material. The vertical garden located downstairs not only lures customers into the basement but also signifies a departure from the monochromatic space of gray and white in the upper space.

Toby's Estate Coffee

125 North 6th Street, Brooklyn, NY, 11249 USA

Studio : nemaworkshop

© Vincent Chih-Chieh Chin

From the exterior, the space is regarded as a stage elevated from the street. The entrance into the space follows a ramp, which leads the guest to a wood bar with marble top, designed to maximize the social interaction between the customer and barista.

Kafé Nordic

29 Itaewon-ro 54ga-gil, Yongsan-gu, Seoul, South Korea

Studio：Nordic Bros. Design Community

The name "Kafé Nordic" comes from the Swedish word for "café" and the English "Nordic". Classical wood flooring was applied to the hall, with 27 custom patterns covering part of the space. The use of emeco, flototto, hay, ton chairs and tables helped create a dynamic space.

toilet

Café Craft

24 rue des Vinaigriers, 75010 Paris, France

Studio : POOL

© Samuel Kirszenbaum

Café Craft is a café positioned as a workplace for freelancers. To imbue the minimalistic business style, the contrast of black and white was incorporated into the brand identity. The iron fences not only divide different dining areas, but also decorate the walls. The wooden and tile floorings divide the space into casual and business areas, enabling customers to relax during coffee break.

Kofemolka Café

Karachevskaya St., 12/3, Orel 302001, Russia

Design : Dmitry Neal

The coffee house interior is divided into two zones: the entrance hall which includes the bar and stools at the windows, and a hall with big tables for big companies of guests. For the interior, turquoise and white have been used as the main colors. The tone of the interior is better balanced by bright colored shutters and countertops with active ashen texture. The main role in the setting is played by the plywood which is a basic material for carved decorative compositions on the walls, natural plants and mirrors that spice up the second hall.

Peggy Guggenheim Café

Palazzo Venier dei Leoni, Dorsoduro 701-704, 30123 Venice, Italy

Studio : Hangar Design Group

Palazzo Venier dei Leoni was once the home of art collector Peggy Guggenheim. The studio reorganized the path leading visitors through the cafeteria, while emphasizing the access to the temporary exhibitions. The chromatic scale consisting of the white of the walls, of the travertine marble and Istrian stone inserts, or even the furniture, is functional to take advantage of the natural light to create the continuity with the open space outside.

Kahve Café by Enflux

1822 West 1st Avenue, Vancouver, BC, Canada

Studio : Johannes Torpe Studios

Design: Eitaro Hirota

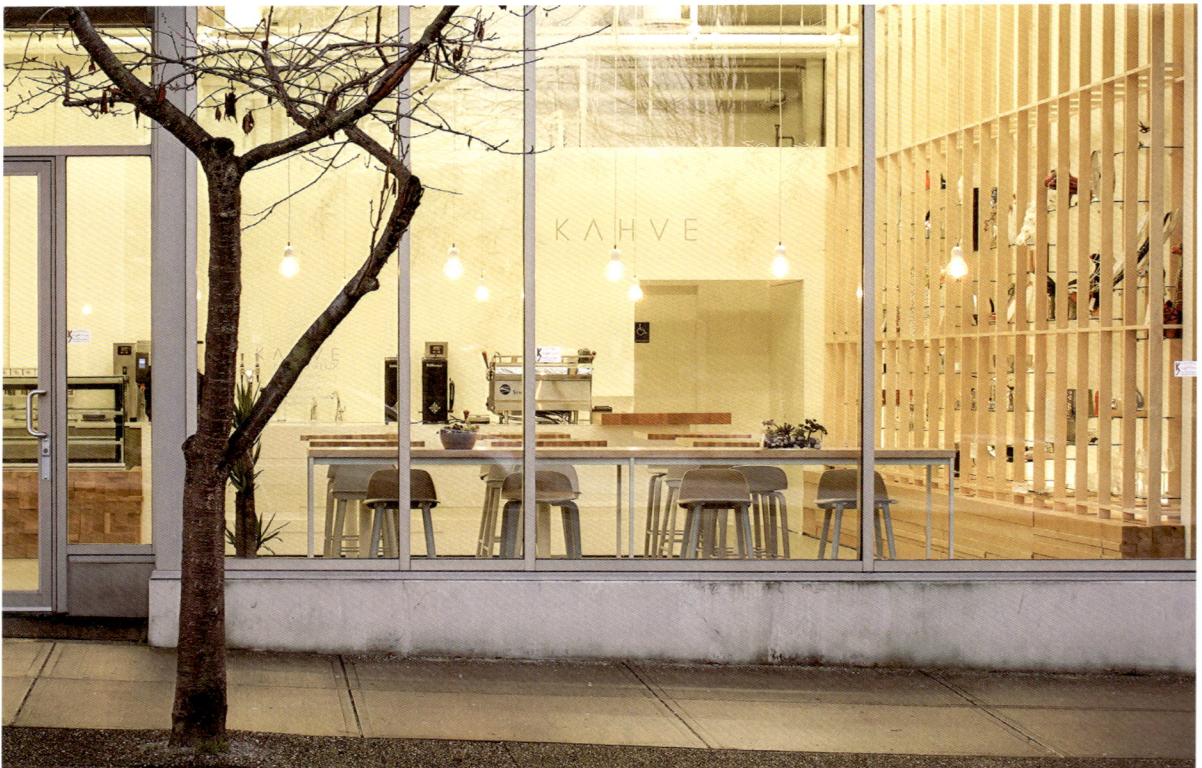

Kahve is a cafe brand opened in the late 2015 by Enflux, a retailer offering modern lifestyle and household goods in Vancouver. The space is light and airy with clean lines, quiet colors and textures. Wood elements are used to create a sense of calm and balance. The wood framed display wall, crafted with Japanese joinery similar to the Machiya wooden lattices, celebrates the cross cultural identity of the locale and highlights the dual positioning of the place: being both a café and a showroom.

Minister Café

Ratajczaka 34, 61-815 Poznań, Poland

Studio : Ostecx Créative

Design : Sébastien Ploszaj

Minister is a private label of Ministry of Brewery in Poznan, Poland. After developing the packaging of Minister Beer, Ostecx Créative was asked to create a consistent brand idenfity and interior design of its newly established brand Minister Café. The visuals were based on the retro feel the word "minister" gives to customers. The bowler hat was used as the main element of the logo.

© Piotr Wręga

Mumin Kaffe

Fabianinkatu 29, 00100 Helsinki, Finland

Studio : Bond

Design : Aleksi Hautamäki, Elina Vuorinen

Mumin Kaffe is not only a tempting place for kids but is also designed to be a place adults could enjoy. Its interior design was inspired by elements from Moomin stories: the paneling of the blue counter resembles the Moomin house and the backrests of the green sofas mirror the Lonely Mountains. The Moomin characters themselves are not the main focus of the space, but are used instead as playful details throughout the interior.

FUEL Café at Chesapeake

6100 North Western Avenue, Oklahoma City, OK 73118, USA

Studio : Elliott + Associates Architects

Design : Rand Elliott, Bill Yen, Miho Kolliopoulos

© Scott McDonald, Hedrich Blessing

With the elements of soft sunlight, colorful crayons and dynamic rainbows in mind, the designers created a fresh and crisp interior space featuring astonishing fluorescent lighting. In this way, the design displays a space that is liquid with colors as if you are dining inside a watercolor painting. The lighting colors was chosen in accord with the food the café provides. The fluorescence combined with the straight trajectory conveys a sense of fiesta and calm.

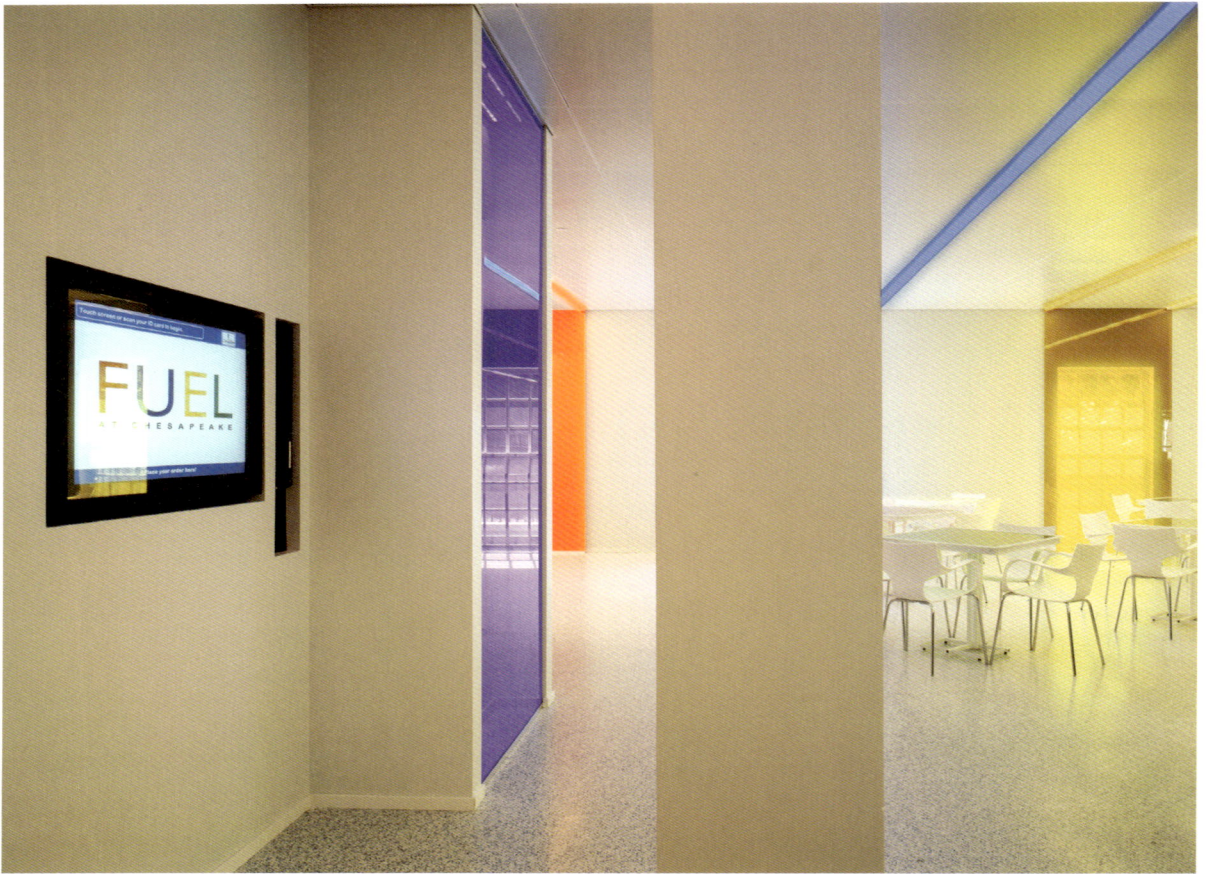

INDEX

ACKNOWLEDGEMENTS

We would like to thank all the designers and contributors who have been involved in the production of this book; their contributions have been indispensable to its creation. We would also like to express our gratitude to all the producers for their invaluable opinions and assistance throughout this project. And to the many others whose names are not credited but have made helpful suggestions, we thank you for your continuous support.

FUTURE PARTNERSHIPS:

If you wish to participate in SendPoints' future projects and publications, please send your website or portfolio to
editor01@sendpoints.cn.

ISBN 978-988-79284-5-4

9 789887 928454